# THE ALEISTER CROWLEY SCRAPBOOK

THE METHOD OF SCIENCE

THE EQUINOX

THE AIM OF RELIGION

# THE
# ALEISTER
# CROWLEY
# SCRAPBOOK

by
Sandy Robertson

# W. Foulsham & Co. Ltd

London • New York • Toronto • Cape Town •
Sydney

Dedicated to Janine LaPerch, velvet-tongued
vampire princess of Los Angeles.

W. Foulsham & Company Limited
Yeovil Road, Slough, Berkshire, SL1 4JH

ISBN 0-572-01456-2

Printed in Great Britain by
St Edmundsbury Press Limited, Bury St Edmunds, Suffolk

# Contents

*Above*: Crowley in
his Jermyn Street flat,
London circa 1943.

*Opposite title page*:
Cover design of
Crowley's occult
periodical, *The
Equinox*.

# Foreword

The key to Aleister Crowley is simple: from childhood to the end of his life, he was in the grip of a ravenous, unsatisfied appetite for recognition. He had no doubt whatever that he deserved recognition; to begin with, he was quite certain that he was one of England's greatest poets. Speaking of the county of his birth, he writes in his autobiography: 'It has been remarked a strange coincidence that one small county should have given England her two greatest poets – for one must not forget Shakespeare.' It sounds like a quip – for that is what Crowley intended – but the underlying conviction was deadly serious.

But fate was to play Crowley an extremely unkind trick. For the first forty eight years of his life he made tremendous efforts to achieve recognition. He published his 'collected works' in his early twenties; he persuaded someone to write a book declaring him the greatest man of his generation; he indulged in every possible kind of self-advertisement. And the British public remained unaware of his existence. Then, quite suddenly, he became a household name when the magazine *John Bull* dubbed him 'the wickedest man in the world', and ran headlines like THE KING OF DEPRAVITY, A HUMAN BEAST and A MAN WE'D LIKE TO HANG. The scandal was all about an 'Abbey' he had founded in Sicily, where dishes of heroin were left around for anyone to help themselves from, where the children were allowed to watch the grown-ups having sex, and where 'magical rituals' involved the sacrifice of animals and a woman being penetrated by a goat. (The goat apparently disliked it, and Crowley cut its throat.) At first Crowley was delighted with his 'fame.' Then it gradually dawned on him that *nothing* he could ever do could now make the British take him seriously. The world had finally noticed his existence – and reacted with a cry of disgust, as if it had trodden on a slug. And so for the last twenty years of his life, Crowley remained, in effect, as 'unknown' as he had ever been. He died a tired and disappointed man.

His contemporaries felt that it served him right. And this, on the whole, is the view that also emerges from the biography written two years after his death in 1947. *The Great Beast* by John Symonds. In the sixties, this suddenly changed. If he had still been alive, he would – as Symonds remarks – undoubtedly have become the patron saint of the Hippies and flower children. When the Beatles included his portrait on the cover of their Sergeant Pepper record, they were paying tribute to an archetypal rebel, the man who went through his life making rude gestures at authority.

Now undoubtedly, all this does Crowley less than justice. It is true that he could be an extremely nasty man, that he was totally self-centred, nursed lifelong grudges, and had a sadistic sense of humour. But, as he once told Frank Harris, he was, for all his 'rottenness', a great magician. He took himself very seriously indeed as a mystic, a yogi and a student of occultism. And anyone who reads his classic on yoga, *Book Four*, or his *Gospel According to St. Bernard Shaw* (recently published as *Crowley on Christ*) will have to agree that he had a keen mind and impressive learning. And although he may not have been quite the Messiah he always believed (he was convinced that Crowleyanity would replace Christianity after his death), his firm instinct about human freedom and the undiscovered powers of the human mind make him an exhilarating thinker.

Crowley's problem, of course, was that he was born in the midst of the Victorian age, into a family of Plymouth Brothers who regarded sex as horribly sinful. He spent the rest of his life violently reacting against this view, and preaching – and practising – the gospel of total sexual freedom. In an age when we take this for granted, he seems to be as absurd as Don Quixote charging at windmills. There was also in his make-up a strong element of the bully Flashman in *Tom Brown's Schooldays*. All this makes his life a kind of moral fable on the dangers of the pitfalls of selfishness and exhibitionism. The result, of course, is that his life and works will be studied long after most of the 'moral reformers' of the 20th century are forgotten. And that, in itself, would undoutedly have given that incorrigible egoist enormous satisfaction.

Colin Wilson.

# Introduction

Who – indeed what – was Aleister Crowley? Magus, poet, sexual athlete, mountaineer, traitor, big-game hunter, chess expert, drug fiend, corrupter of souls and Prophet of a New Aeon – he has been described as all these things. Born a member of the ultra-strict Plymouth Brethren, he ended up named by the gutter press as 'The Wickedest Man In The World'. He was the founder of a religion and yet wrote the vilest pornography. He pursued women relentlessly but practised homosexual magick. He advocated strength of will yet died a penniless heroin addict in a Hastings boarding house. He was an enigma, even to himself.

I first heard of Crowley about twenty years ago: I recall that, having spotted some sneering reference to him in a trashy paperback on black magic, I asked my father why this man was so hated. His answer, in the form of a scowl and an indication that this was *not* a subject that anyone who wanted to remain sane ought to pursue, set me off on a wild trail that has persisted to this day.

Since that moment when I first became fascinated with the legend of The Beast, there have, of course, been changes in the popularity of the Crowley name. The hippies, those weak-willed lotus eaters whom Crowley would have despised, mistakenly saw in his rugged individualism some forerunner of their own crapulous creed. Many rock musicians, including The Beatles, The Rolling Stones, David Bowie, Jimmy Page and Graham Bond, were caught up in his spell at some time. His books, formerly available at jumble-sale rates, now command amazingly high prices at auction.

There have been at least half-a-dozen biographies of Crowley but despite all the attention I suspect that the man-in-the-street's opinion has changed little. If he has heard of Crowley at all it's as 'England's Worst Man', the leering devil-worshipper, according to the lurid descriptions of his parents drawn from dimly remembered articles in the *Sunday Express* of long ago.

Hopefully, this volume may change at least a few opinions. Dear reader, I give you Aleister Crowley, Alastor de Kerval, To Mega Therion, the Wanderer Of The Waste, Frater Perdurabo, The Great Beast 666: a Hell of a Holy Guru indeed!

Sandy Robertson,
London, 1988 e.v.

# The World of Aleister Crowley

**"I may be a Black Magician, but I'm a bloody great one." Crowley's diary, 1923.**

*Opposite*: Crowley as a schoolboy. Despite the happy expression, his childhood was not an easy one. He attended several schools, experiencing some brutal treatment, and suffered a nervous breakdown.

Edward Alexander Crowley was born on October 12th, 1875 to a family of apparently paradoxical beliefs: they were not only members of an extreme teetotal sect of the Plymouth Brethren but also the brewers of Crowley's Ales! In fact, Crowley's father had made his fortune from the beer trade and retired to Leamington for a life of undisturbed study of the scriptures: the resultant atmosphere, although the youngster railed against it later, surely having a strong influence on Crowley's eventual desire to lead his own religion, albeit an anti-Christian one.

Aleister (he changed his name from Edward to avoid sharing it with his hated father, who died when he was eleven) grew to loathe the 'Darbyite' creed of the Plymouth Brethren in which his family believed, chiefly because of his experiences at the hands of the cruel headmaster of the special sect school he attended in Cambridge. In 1892 he went to public school in Malvern, where 'sodomy was the rule' and his room mate turned out to be selling himself as a homosexual prostitute to the other boys. So he had himself transferred to Tonbridge, where (having already been initiated into the joys of sex at fourteen by an obliging maid back home) he caught gonorrhoea from a streetwalker.

He seems to have been just as nasty as most little boys; torturing a cat in several horrid ways to see if it really *did* have nine lives and nearly killing himself with a gigantic homemade firework. Yet Crowley somehow ended up studying at Cambridge, developing an interest in Alpine climbing and a taste for good food and drink and luxuriously-bound volumes of poetry, sometimes by Shelley and Keats but more often his own efforts in the style of Swinburne. He coupled lustily with friends of both sexes (including H C J Pollitt, a gay friend of Beardsley's) and lent his support to weird causes.

And yet he was still unsatisfied . . .

In 1896 in a Stockholm hotel Crowley had what Colin Wilson would describe as a 'peak experience' – one of those flashes of insight, ecstatic in nature, into the wonderful possibilities of life. This led him to search for a means of realizing these possibilities but it was not until two years later, when he was introduced to one George Cecil Jones, that he started out on the path towards magical enlightenment that was to occupy him for the rest of his life.

Jones was a member of that strange organisation known as The Hermetic Order Of The Golden Dawn, which, although it claimed great antiquity, was really part of the irrationalist

*Above*: The Beast in the robes of a Golden Dawn initiate.

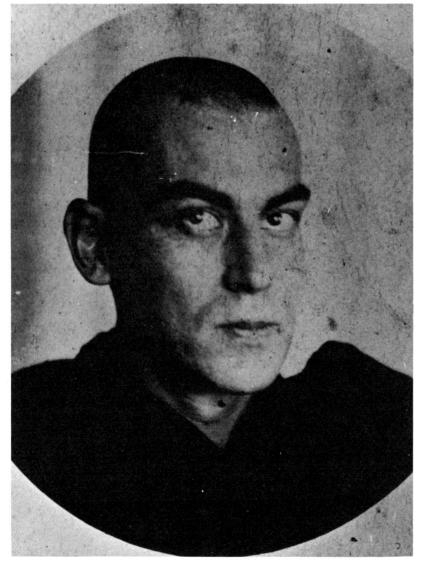

*Left*: Allan Bennett, who introduced Crowley to yoga when they were both members of the Golden Dawn, later became a Buddhist. 'The Adeptus I.A.' (opposite) refers to Bennett's Golden Dawn motto, Iehi Aour.

The Adeptus I.A. C.H.A.B.A.Mc.G.
Ac.1896

= Al Ayn ben Ayt = Ananda Metteya =

"Come in Peace - O beatified and divine One! - to a body glorified and perfected ; Herald of the gods. Knowing his speech among the living! Pass Thou through every region in Amenta into the place wherein the god dwelleth - because thou comest in Peace. provided with thy Wealth."
Stele of ABU. IInd Dyn.

upsurge of magic and decadence of the late 19th century that had exploded into being as a reaction against the increasing humdrum mechanisation of the age. Nevertheless, The Golden Dawn was a route to occult knowledge and boasted such members as that novelist of the bizarre, Arthur Machen, and the poet W B Yeats.

Crowley advanced rapidly in the Order, finding favour with its head, MacGregor Mathers, and another member named Allan Bennett. In his flat in Chancery Lane young Aleister had constructed both White and Black Temples: the White was lined with mirrors, while the Black had an altar supported by a statue of a negro standing on his hands as well as a skeleton to which he resolutely sacrificed sparrows!

The Golden Dawn soon found itself in a fragmented state

*Left*: S.L.M Mathers, the Head of the Golden Dawn, with whom Crowley was to quarrel.

due to Crowley. In 1900 he became entitled to the magical Grade of Adeptus Minor, having completed the necessary course of study, but the London controllers of the Golden Dawn didn't approve of Crowley's homosexual dabblings and refused him advancement. He went to Mathers in Paris, who performed the ceremony personally, thus outraging the London members. In the ensuing uproar, members resigned, Mathers was deposed and Crowley tried to get hold of the Order's property on behalf of Mathers. There were even astral attacks, and in the end the police were called in.

Crowley tired of the dispute and spent the next few years travelling the globe: Mexico, Egypt, India, France, Ceylon. He also married Rose Kelly, sister of the painter who was to become Sir Gerald Kelly, R.A., travelling with her to Egypt. It was in Cairo in March 1904, that the most important event of Crowley's life occurred.

On three consecutive days he took down dictation from a discarnate entity called Aiwass, which Crowley believed to be his Holy Guardian Angel. The resulting text was called *The Book Of The Law*, prophesying the Age Of Horus, The Crowned And Conquering Child, and signalling that a new era had begun for mankind. One of the key principles of the new age was 'Do What Thou Wilt Shall Be The Whole Of The Law'; misinterpreted by many as a licence to go wild and indulge one's whims, failing to see the real meaning was that one should discover one's true will. 'Love Is The Law, Love Under Will' and 'Every Man And Every Woman Is A Star' were the two other main principles.

Aleister Crowley wrote to Mathers informing him that he, Crowley, was now top dog in the magical world; but though he won the demonic duel which is said to have resulted, Crowley lost interest in the occult for the next few years and succumbed to marital bliss.

Of course, Crowley occupied himself in other ways in those intervening years. In 1905 he was involved in a disastrous attempt to climb Kangchenjunga, the then unassailed Himalayan peak, with a man named Guillarmod who had tried to ascend the equally dangerous K2 in his company on a previous expedition. There were deaths, from which Crowley exonerated himself, while Guillarmod accused him of cowardice. Then he trekked across China, dragging his wife and child with him. He visited Canada and America, leaving his family behind, and it was not until he arrived back in England that he learnt of the death of his daughter of typhus in Rangoon.

In 1907 Crowley started his own magical organisation, the Silver Star or Argenteum Astrum. Later, he began to publish its official organ: a twice-yearly bulky volume called *The Equinox*, so-dubbed because it appeared at the vernal and autumnal equinoxes. The vast majority of the contents was written by Crowley himself. Why all this sudden magical activity? After all, he now had a new baby girl to dote on. However, his interest in all things magical had been rekindled when one day, while rummaging around in the attic, he had re-discovered the fateful manuscript of *The Book Of The Law*.

*Below*: 1902 expedition to Chogo Ri (K2). Crowley is seated, middle row, right. He was later to be involved in an ill-fated attempt on another mountain, Kangchenjunga.

Divorced from Rose in 1909, by which time she had become an alcoholic, Crowley was free to take drugs, pursue women, write poetry, indulge in magick and even to travel to Russia with a dancing troupe he called The Ragged Rag-Time Girls! In 1912 he was contacted by the head of a German magical order called the OTO, or Ordo Templi Orientis, (Order of the Templars of the East) and accused of publishing the secret of their IXth degree. Crowley was mystified, but after discussion it transpired that a reference in one of his books had caused the OTO to assume Crowley was involved in sex magic, which they used in their rituals. It was not long

*Below*: Aleister Crowley with his first wife Rose, whom he was to divorce because of her alcoholism, and their daughter, Lola Zaza.

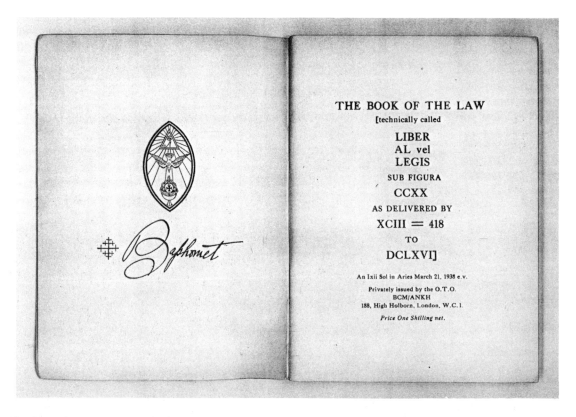

THE BOOK OF THE LAW

[technically called

LIBER
AL vel
LEGIS

SUB FIGURA

CCXX

AS DELIVERED BY

XCIII ═ 418

TO

DCLXVI]

An Ixii Sol in Aries March 21, 1938 e.v.

Privately issued by the O.T.O.
BCM/ANKH
188, High Holborn, London, W.C.1.

*Price One Shilling net.*

before it was agreed that he ought to be the Order's UK head.

During the First World War Crowley published anti-British propaganda in the USA, which he later claimed was done on the basis of *reductio ad absurdum*; that is, his writings apparently in support of the German cause were actually ridiculing it and were therefore really to Great Britain's benefit! Few took him at his word and the description 'traitor' was added to his worsening reputation in Britain. After the conflict he returned to Europe with his new Scarlet Woman, Leah Hirsig, who bore him a child, Poupée, and in 1920 he set up his notorious Abbey Of Thelema at Cefalù, Sicily.

And Poupée, too, died. Crowley was heartbroken. He travelled between Paris and London and the Abbey, trying to cure his (by now raging) heroin and cocaine habits. He wrote a novel, *The Diary Of A Drug Fiend*, which was condemned by the press, perhaps unfairly as it is simply a disguised story of his Abbey and how a young couple are cured of their drug problems. It would hardly encourage anyone into addiction, so awful is its description of the pains of withdrawal.

When a young undergraduate named Raoul Loveday died

*Above*: The first commercially issued edition of *The Book of the Law*.

from drinking impure water at the Abbey, his wife went home and sold her story to the *Sunday Express*. For a while, the papers were filled with scandalous stories of the 'black magic' rituals and other goings-on at the Abbey, and Crowley's name was well and truly blackened. At the same time came the ascent of the Mussolini regime, with its hatred of all secret societies except its own, and The Beast was expelled from Sicily. From here on Aleister Crowley's career took a darker turn.

Though some of his friends stuck by him and tried to vindicate his name, the going wasn't easy. A mathematician named Norman Mudd published a pamphlet refuting the slurs of the Beaverbrook newspapers: he ended up destitute, abandoned by Crowley, finally killing himself by drowning. No British printer would be associated with Crowley's *magnum opus*, *Magick In Theory And Practice*, and it had to be produced in Paris. He was deported from France for no good reason other than vicious rumour.

Crowley's fortunes continued to decline. Back in Britain, he began to write books for the Mandrake Press but the booksellers refused to stock his 'autohagiography', *The Confessions Of Aleister Crowley*. When he was invited to

*Below*: The order of service pamphlet for Crowley's funeral. Note the incorrect birthdate.

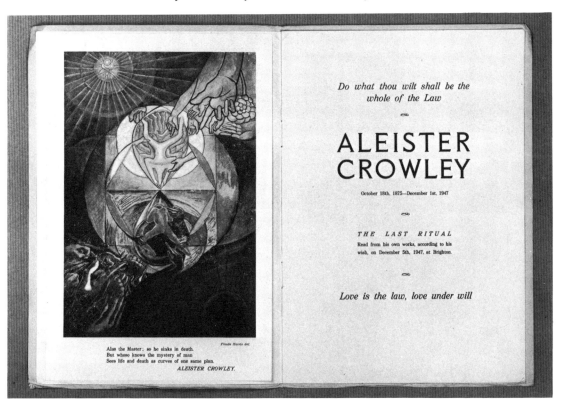

Alas the Master; so he sinks in death.
But whoso knows the mystery of man
Sees life and death as curves of one same plan.
ALEISTER CROWLEY.

*Frieda Harris del.*

Do what thou wilt shall be the whole of the Law

# ALEISTER CROWLEY

October 18th, 1875—December 1st, 1947

THE LAST RITUAL
Read from his own works, according to his wish, on December 5th, 1947, at Brighton.

Love is the law, love under will

*Autobiography of a Remarkable Man*

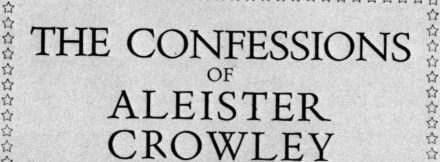

# THE CONFESSIONS
## OF
# ALEISTER CROWLEY

## TO BE ISSUED IN SIX VOLUMES
### at Two Guineas a Volume

Each Volume will be approximately 240 pp., Imperial 8vo,
beautifully printed in Poliphilus type on White Japon Vellum,
bound full Buckram with bevelled boards and gold design

### Volumes I and II will be issued immediately
The remaining volumes will appear next year

☆

## THE MANDRAKE PRESS
*41 Museum Street, London, W.C.1*

Autumn 1929

*Opposite*: Cover of the rare prospectus for the Mandrake Press edition of Crowley's *Confessions*. In the end, just two volumes were issued, the third only reaching proof stage.

read a paper on the subject of Gilles De Rais at Oxford University Poetry Society, he was banned by the Chaplain. After winning a court case for a small libel committed by a bookshop, he tried the same thing on a bigger scale by suing the painter Nina Hamnett over comments about him in her book *Laughing Torso*. He lost, with costs found against him and was declared bankrupt.

For the remainder of his life the Wanderer Of The Waste wandered mainly through England. Followers in the USA kept him supplied with life's little luxuries during the war, and similarly afterwards when he ended up in Hastings, still mentally sharp but hopelessly addicted to enormous shots of heroin.

He died on December 1st 1947, and his funeral took place four days later at Brighton Crematorium, with readings from his works as he had desired. The papers were suitably shocked by the moving ceremony. The local council promised to take steps to see that such a thing never happened again.

Crowley wanted to be thought of as evil and enjoyed the reputation of being The Wickedest Man In The World, but found that, unfortunately, he couldn't control this image or simply shake it off when it became inconvenient. What did others think of him? Gerald Yorke, his friend and indefatigable collector of his works, wrote, 'Whatever Crowley was, he was not a charlatan. He believed, he worked, he suffered, he had power. He failed to put over the religion of Thelema in his lifetime, which, considering its nature, is not surprising. The Christian world regards him as one of the Devil's Contemplatives. His few friends will not see his like again; but his still fewer disciples mourn the passing of a Magus.' (*The Occult Observer*, Vol 1, No 2, Summer 1949).

Lance Sieveking, the author, said in his autobiography *The Eye Of The Beholder*: 'I am convinced in my own mind that Aleister Crowley knew a lot of things. But they are things that I, personally, do not wish to know.'

And finally I append the text of the late Alan Burnett-Rae's *A Memoir Of 666*, which has only been previously available in a limited edition from Victor Hall's Victim Press. Burnett-Rae's article gives an interesting insight into the everyday life of The Beast in the 1930s, and I make no apologies for reprinting it in full.

## A MEMOIR OF 666 *by Alan Burnett-Rae*

My knowledge of that strange man Aleister Crowley dates from 1934, continuing intermittently until I joined up in 1940. For a period of some weeks he was a tenant of mine in Welbeck Street, and I saw him almost daily, often for the bootless purpose of asking for the rent or remonstrating with him for disturbing the peace of the house. At other times he lived elsewhere. I remember visiting him in Bloomsbury, Chelsea and Wimbledon. Our relations were, on the whole, friendly.

The first occasion on which I met Crowley was in the Mayfair Hotel one Sunday afternoon late in May, or early in June, 1934. A certain Dr. Alexander Cannon, sometime Head (if that be the title) of Colney Hatch Asylum was giving a lecture and a demonstration of hypnotic phenomena in the hotel and a number of invitation cards had been distributed to various persons, many of whom were doctors, among them my father, then in practice in Harley Street. He was not particularly interested and I asked him for the invitations and went to the hotel with my mother and sister.

Cannon had recently written a book entitled *The Invisible Influence* which had caused a considerable stir. It concerned occult matters and had led some influential people to a conclusion not altogether favourable to Dr. Cannon, and casting doubt on his fitness to be in charge of a lunatic asylum. By some chance I had read the book and it was this that made me attend the meeting at the Mayfair. After thirty-five years it is not easy to remember exactly what was said, but I do recall that an attempt was made to "levitate" a young lady, said to be a daughter of the famous dancer Nijinski. To my disappointment, but not surprise, the experiment failed; although Cannon invited me to place my hand under her ankle and test the weight of the leg and, indeed, it seemed strangely supple and light. The girl was certainly in some kind of trance. Cannon later told me, when I approached him with some questions, that the experiment would have succeeded had it been feasible to strip the girl in the main lounge of the hotel. The weight of the clothes, he said, was fatal to success. While other questions were being asked, a large man with a heavy face and what remained of grey hairs, clad in a brown tweed, knickerbocker suit which matched the colour of his face, rose and asked a question in a rather contentious voice. He was answered in kind and a rather sharp argument soon developed with Cannon. I recall that at last some of the audience began to shout "Sit down" and, at this, I myself stood up and asked why the unknown's question should not be fairly answered. The meeting ended shortly afterwards and tea was served.

In the course of tea, while chatting with my mother and sister, I observed the man in brown tweed making his way over the lounge in our direction.

He came up and thanked me for my intervention on his behalf and made some observations, more or less uncomplimentary to Dr. Cannon. I talked to him for some minutes about the lecture and the levitation, and while so engaged I noticed my mother and sister rise and leave.

*Opposite*: Crowley as Burnett-Rae must have known him.

They later said they could not endure the proximity of the man any longer and wondered how I could endure it either! They had never seen him before.

I believe I offered to drive Dr. Cannon back to his house. At all events he asked me to visit him at his new asylum at Bexley Heath (he had then left Colney Hatch) and this invitation I accepted with some interesting results. He told me that the man in brown was the notorious Aleister Crowley, a would-be Black Magician, drug addict, author of strange books and a man of stranger reputation.

Some time later, perhaps two years, I had become the possessor of a house in Welbeck Street divided into some eight or nine flatlets. I occupied one of these and let the others to various tenants. I employed a Belgian steward, his wife, his son and a housemaid.

This brought me in a comfortable income and allowed me leisure to interest myself in various subjects which had attracted me, including the Occult. A person I got to know at this time was a West Indian negro named Rollo Ahmed, who had written a book about the negro struggle for what are now called 'human rights'. He was also interested in Magic and voodoo, and claimed to be an "adept" and I had watched him try various experiments of an inconclusive nature. One day he rang me up and said that if I had a flat to let he would bring along a friend of his whom he described as "a very highly evolved personality" who would be a satisfactory tenant in every respect.

When they arrived I had no difficulty in recognising the 'highly evolved personality' as Aleister Crowley.

He was wearing the identical knickerbocker suit of two years before and that face was unforgettable. Much has been said about his teeth, which apparently he had filed into points (*à la vampire*), but I did not notice this detail, only that they were widely spaced, suggesting the black keys on a piano board.

I reminded him of our previous meeting, which he recalled; I reminded him also of an occasion when he had visited Oxford when I was 'up' to give a lecture on Gilles de Rais, the fourteenth century occultist and how the proctors had refused permission for the lecture to be given, threatening to 'send down' the undergraduate sponsor if it took place. I agreed to let him have a flatlet and he moved in, agreeing to a weekly rent. Of course, I know now that I was rash. I should have obtained references; I might have known that Ahmed was no reliable guarantor of anything, or anybody, that Crowley was an undischarged bankrupt and one or two other things that a prudent man of affairs would have made it his business to find out. But I was twenty-five years of age at the time and thought more of how interesting it would be to find out more about this notorious personality — 'highly evolved' or otherwise. He moved in that day.

I was out of town for a while after this and it was on my return that the steward reported to me that the new tenant was making rather a nuisance of himself by burning powerful incense. This was beyond a doubt; I could perceive it myself. Further, he was most exacting in his demands. The Belgian steward's son Adolphe (soon to change his name to Jack for political and social reasons!) was constantly being sent on errands to purchase strange foods and drinks. Pigs' trotters, I remember, were one of Crowley's favourite dishes, usually ordered at impossible

23

hours. In the matter of drink, I remember he was remarkably abstemious for a man who had the reputation of indulging in every conceivable vice. When I knew him rather better and asked him in for a drink, I offered brandy. I had refilled his glass once or twice when to my amazement he toppled off his chair and slumped to the ground as if unconscious. A woman friend of his, the middle-aged widow of a naval officer, was with us and when we had got Crowley back into his armchair she explained that he should never be given spirits. He had asthma, recurrent malaria, this, that and the other afflictions, acquired over the years, which made him over susceptible to drink. I did not make the same mistake again.

The steward also informed me that Crowley had not settled his account since he came, that his telephone calls were frequent and lengthy, and no doubt expensive and finally that strange noises in his flat were to be heard during the night. Of the latter ground of complaint I had no doubt after the steward aroused me at about two in the morning and bade me listen, shortly after my return to London. There certainly were sounds of infernal screaming, shouting and general commotion on the third floor.

"It's Mr. Crowley beating up Mrs. –" explained Verhoeven quite simply.

"Well, go up and tell him to desist. I'll give him notice in the morning."

"After you, sir," was the reply. So up I got and having reached the third floor flat whence the din proceeded, I knocked and called Crowley's name loudly, demanding admittance, Verhoeven standing by in close support.

The row stopped abruptly and after a few moments the door opened and the face of the widow appeared. Although it must have been her screams that had aroused the house, she apologetically explained that poor Aleister had had one of his recurring nightmares but that he now felt better and it would not occur again. She was obviously opposed to my entering the flat and I did not insist, but intimated that I had had enough and would see him in the morning, when I had every intention of giving him notice to leave.

The pair anticipated me and called at my flat on the ground floor before I was even dressed. They appeared perfectly amicable with each other and deeply contrite about what they assured me was an unfortunate accident. He did have nightmares, he said. He had not had one for some time now and he doubted whether he would have another for a long time to come. I accepted this explanation, although it was an obvious fabrication, and then told him that I expected to receive the rent which had not been forthcoming. There was a prolonged story about assets in America; about a trust fund; and, finally, a promise to settle the account. Indeed on the next day he did settle it – in cash, and I have little doubt that it was the lady's money that he handed over. I asked him to abate the nuisance of the incense and not make such continual demands on the staff and to these requests he agreed.

As far as the asthma was concerned, I do not doubt his story. I noticed a strange-looking machine in his room which at first I took to be a dictaphone, but which he told me was a gadget which enabled him to breathe when the fit came upon him.

This machine, the brown suit, the incense burner and some books seemed to comprise his entire property. One day he took one of these books, opened it, inscribed my name therein and presented it to me. This was his *Equinox of the Gods*, as the gold inlaid title announced. There was some cabalistic device, also gilt inlaid, on the cover with a hexagram, some numerals and the inscription

"Sigillum Sanctum fraternitatis A∴A∴. The title informed one that it was the official organ of the A∴A∴ (meaning unknown to the author) and that this was also the official organ of the O.T.O. ("Ordo Templi Orientis").

The general obscurity of the writing together with the signs and symbols, the use of Latin, Greek, Hebrew and even ancient Egyptian terminology was typical of the man's ordinary conversation which frequently provoked me to impatient protest. At other times, however, he interested me by anecdotes of his travels which had been world-wide, including notable ascents of mountains and explorings in many lands. Tales of the buried cities of Ceylon and South America, of the Russia of the Tsars and of the pre-1914 world were of real interest to me, and at these times I would enjoy his company. And then out would come some irritatingly outrageous statement such as "It was there that I materialised the Sylphs in 1906, of course!" and I would remember a pressing appointment and leave. It was inevitable that such a man should have tried Yoga and Crowley claimed to have attained "Dhyana", described by him in his book as a "tremendous spiritual experience, in which the subject and object of meditation unites with excessive violence in binding brilliance and music of a kind to which earthly harmony affords no parallel". But the fact is that Crowley did not look like an ascetic who had by great self-discipline mastered a difficult and exhausting art or science. Although not more than sixty-one at this time, he was overweight, clumsy in his movements, asthmatic and generally unfit. Of course, it is probable that he was, as he claimed to have been, a fine athlete at one time, but as he also claimed to have been a drug addict and general bon viveur, these things presumably militated against fitness. Whenever I walked along the street with him he maintained a very sedate pace for a man who claimed to have held world speed records for walking uphill at heights over 16,000 feet. However, all that was thirty-six years before and much must have happened in the meantime.

According to his own works, and supported by his conversation, his great interests in life were a perverse sort of mysticism and Sex. As to the first, it seemed simply to consist of a cult of blasphemy in which he saw himself as a type of Anti-Christ. I recall how, whenever he passed any kind of clergyman in the street, he would always utter some kind of gibberish and make a gesture with his hand which, unlikely as it may have been, was rather like crossing his fingers. On one occasion my father the doctor, came to visit me and, on learning that Crowley lived in the house, expressed horror. It seems he had heard a story from one of his patients to the effect that Crowley and his disciples had broken into a Church in Brussels by night and celebrated a "Mass" where the altar was a naked woman on her hands and knees. I think he told me that the patient had been one of the participants in these on-goings and was now repenting his sins with a nervous breakdown. My father was almost equally indignant with me for laughing at this tale as for harbouring the man.

It became known to me that his father, Edward Crowley, was a member of the Exclusive Plymouth Brothers, but Crowley denied what everyone naturally suggested: that his present attitude was a reaction from an excessively strict religious parentage. He said his father, although a keen proselyte, never allowed his religion to "interfere with natural affection!" It was the people who brought him up after his father's death who caused his mental attitude to be concentrated in an almost pathological hatred of the Christian religion, and those who professed it. In so far as he had a religion, I suppose it was 'Crowleianity' and he was its Prophet and King under many and various titles.

The names by which he went in his time were legion. At Welbeck Street in 1936–7 letters arrived addressed to "Sir Aleister Crowley". At other times he had been Lord Boleskine, the Comte de St. Germain and other entitled gentlemen, quite apart from being the Great Beast 666, Priest of the Princes, etc. He always asserted that he was of "Earth's First Blood", an aristocrat and a genius. He complained or boasted when reduced to poverty, or relative poverty, that he had never been brought up to work and was therefore now unable to. Nevertheless, he three times attempted to repair his fortunes by persuading me to back him financially. The first occasion was in December, 1936, when the abdication crisis was at its height and the King was known to be considering abandoning the throne. Crowley called on me very early one morning, and suggested that I should put up some hundreds of pounds to have discs stamped with the words, "We want our King" to be worn in button-holes. He was convinced they would sell at a substantial profit.

I declined this suggestion, but not long after he came out with another. If I would finance a trip to the U.S.A., accompanying him if I chose, and financing some legal proceedings, he could establish a rightful claim to the Headship of Primacy (whatever the title was) to A.M.O.R.C. the initials of the Rosicrucian Order. The rewards would be in the order of millions of dollars, waiting to be claimed by the rightfully entitled, and I was going to sit at his righthand when he came to glory. This suggestion, also, I felt obliged to turn down.

Another Crowleian enterprise was that we should market under his auspices, and with my money, the 'Elixir of Rejuvenation' itself. I had thrown him out by this time as an economic liability and he was living in Hasker Street, Chelsea. None the less, I kept in touch, chiefly because I was consumed with curiosity wondering what on earth he would be up to next. He would not tell me what the Elixir was, but one of his women friends did and if I had ever entertained any belief in it, it was now dissipated. But he had all the literature about it printed. It was in the form of a diary by an unnamed person, but it was obvious that the writer was Crowley himself, although he would not have admitted this as it would have been tantamount to the admission that the Great Beast 666 had recently suffered some decline in sexual potency, and this ran contrary to the very nature of things.

As he had written several books, his mind was always occupied with ideas that he might recoup his fortunes by a last supremely successful book; but he could no longer afford to publish it himself and it seemed no one else would do it now. The name of Simpkin Marshall was often on his tongue in this connection. Perhaps thirty years later he might, in a different climate of opinion, have had more luck in finding a publisher.

Elixir or no elixir, he continued to have women about him and he did not lose interest in that subject. Once he asked me to the Café Royal to meet one of his mistresses and his son. We arrived there and he introduced her by some strange name and, also, "my son, Alistair Ataturk". I failed to see Alistair Ataturk, and Crowley added "Perhaps I should mention that Ataturk is still an inside passenger." I noticed that this was so. This seems to have been the girl who introduced herself to him during the law suit against Nina Hamnett and offered to bear him a child.

Once, before he left Welbeck Street, after I had given a party which he did not attend I went to his flat for some

reason. He was quick to notice that I had a bite on the side of the neck and his eye gleamed with interest. I explained that the lady had been "one of those biting and scratching maniacs". Crowley immediately asked to be introduced at the earliest possible opportunity, and for some days or weeks he never saw me without repeating the request and quoting the words, "your biting and scratching maniac" with relish.

It was in the Café Royal, that he nearly landed himself in serious trouble. Crowley had gone in to the downstair restaurant where unaccompanied women had never been allowed. He saw some trouble going on and went to investigate. Finding the manager was trying to evict a member of the sorority who was declining to leave quietly, Crowley went up to them and said "It's quite all right, manager; this lady is with me."

"I think not, sir," was the reply, "I'm afraid we know her very well."

"Dog!" shouted Crowley and brought down upon the man's head his favourite walking stick which he told me was made from a rhinoceros's penis, strectched by weights and cured in the sun. I was not actually present at this episode but he himself advised me of it, wondering whether the Café Royal would be so parochial and obscurantist as to object to his going there again! I suggested he should let time elapse.

When it became known among my friends and acquaintances that the notorious Beast was to be seen, as it were, on application to the curator, many asked to be introduced. Not all, however. One, the top floor tenant, came to me and, with the utmost seriousness, asked me if I knew what risks I was running by having such a man in the house. I explained that the principal risk was in losing the use of a perfectly good flat without obtaining any rent from it. But he did not mean that. He was genuinely afraid of Crowley's evil influence on those who came near him and declared that he knew someone who had a friend who could testify that someone he knew of had a positive cataract of misfortunes as a result of merely knowing Crowley. He told me he could not himself remain in the house if Satan was to be his fellow-tenant. I contrived to laugh him out of this but he positively refused to meet Aleister face to face.

Others were only too pleased to drop in for a drink when they had been told that the Mage would be there. One fairly senior Civil Servant, from the War Office, who had been at school with me and also with that other 'distinguished public servant' Kim Philby, was with me when Crowley rang down to ask me up for drinks, or with my friends, if I were not alone. My top floor tenant declined point blank, but the War Office man volunteered with enthusiasm, and setting his foot on the first step of the stairs, turned to us and declaimed, "It is a far, far better thing that I do than I have ever done", and led the way up.

I often talked to Crowley alone. I remember once asking him why if, as he was the first to claim, he was a man of outstanding parts, he did not seek fame and reputation, rather than notoriety and more or less general public distrust, in the way he had done for so long.

"What is the use of most fame?" he answered. "I once thought of the Diplomatic Service as a career, but can you tell me now who was our representative at the Sublime Porte, say, eighty years ago?"

"Stratford de Redcliffe," I replied instantly, having some time before read up the Crimean War, inspired by seeing "The Lady with the Lamp" then running in London. He looked somewhat disconcerted but quickly said, "Oh,

well! You know what I mean. No one will remember in a few more years, will they?''

Among the women friends of Aleister Crowley I met, whose names may be remembered more than a generation later, were Nina Hamnett and Betty May.

Nina was the model for the piece of sculpture entitled "Laughing Torso". This I believe dated from many years before and the model, when I met her, although adequate enough physically, did not suggest a Praxitelean goddess. Crowley was friendly towards her and she towards him as far as I could see, in spite of the libel suit he had brought against her and lost, following the publication of her first book.

Far otherwise with Betty May, the "Tiger Woman". She had, it seems, been one of the company assembled at the Temple of Thelema in Sicily in the early twenties and had been the fiancée of the young man whose death there caused scandalous comment and was one of the causes of Aleister's expulsion by the Italian Government, although an inquest had returned a verdict of death by natural causes. The ill-disposed, however, among whom Betty was numbered, ascribed his end to Crowley. The reasons given were always different. The most bizarre that I heard being that the youth contracted some fatal disease after drinking the blood of a sacrificed cat. Judging from the evidence of other writers this is not impossible. The Tiger Woman, at all events appeared to be wholly convinced of the Crowleian guilt and swore to me that he was the murderer of her young friend. She was clearly drunk at the time and the man who introduced me (I think it was at the Fitzroy Tavern) warned me not to let her know that Crowley was living in my house or she might create a scene or come round with a view to assaulting or denouncing him. As it was, she was that night in a most convivial mood, assuring me confidentially that she would one day kill Crowley and, further, that she was herself a witch! I remember that, although by then her hair was turning grey, she had the remains of attractiveness if not beauty. There were one or two other ladies Crowley knew to one of which he was giving a ceremonial bath when he introduced us, and another of hideous appearance whom I recognised as the original of an oil painting by the Master himself, which hung on his wall. He was a painter of no small ability but his work always had a macabre quality. If he might have said, "Evil, be thou my God", he might equally have pronounced that "Truth was Ugliness and Ugliness Truth" as far as art was concerned.

His verse-making or poetry, too, was by no means despicable. He had a great love of words and particularly of names from ancient languages. He always renamed his women followers with titles such as "The Scarlet Woman" or Astroel even as he was Frater Perdurabo himself. I once heard some young fellow recite his "Hymn to Pan" most effectively. Indeed, I have since been told that this hymn or ode was finally recited at Crowley's funeral in the chapel of the Crematorium at Brighton. The introduction to the *Equinox of the Gods* is in the form of a rhymed colloquy between an Adept and an Accolyte.

> "Master! While yet the glory clings
> Declare this mystery magical."

*Opposite*: Betty May, the wife of young Raoul Loveday who died at Crowley's abbey in Sicily. She later spread strange tales about the ritual sacrifices performed there.

Marsyas, the Adept, who seems to be Crowley, has no hesitation in accepting the invitation throughout the remainder of the book, in which he declares a new 'Aeon' of which he was Lord and Prophet. I have mentioned that he was unusually temperate in his use of alcohol and that even a slight excess of spirits would cause him to 'pass out'. The same could not be said of his curries! I was invited to have one of these, prepared by himself, one day just before the war. At the first mouthful I thought I had burned my tongue with caustic acid and reached for the water and thereafter took water with every successive spoonful. Crowley, however, shovelled an enormous plateful away with record speed, fortifying it as he went with chillies and other spices, the sweat pouring down his face, as if he were in a Turkish bath. When he had eaten copiously, he helped himself to more and offered me another plateful but I had had enough, although normally I am fond of curry. He explained that he had learnt about *real* curry in India, Burma and Ceylon, that its object was to produce sweating, and hence a cooling process, also designed to stimulate the system generally in hot climates. He pointed out that this was only one of many cooling processes he was familiar with in these lands and that one of the great points of hospitality was to have one's *partes viriles* lifted up by a maiden attendant, and fanned from below with an exquisitely painted fan. He gave me to infer that in the circles in which he moved and had his being in such countries this was most normal practice. He assured me I would soon get to enjoy such things, as well as curry, once I got out there, to say nothing of the delights of opium, hashish and heroin.

All this was shortly before the war. I was then considering what I should do about some kind of military service and I mentioned this to him and added that I might find myself in curry-eating lands sooner than I might otherwise have expected. "That is no way to go out East," he snorted. "What is this new military obsession that is seizing on evebody? Level of intelligence-military. I am surprised at you!"

I said something to the effect that having mismanaged affairs to the point that another world war was imminent, the only thing left to do was to apply ourselves to the winning of it, should it take place. I reminded him of the fact that he had often complained of dictators and dictatorship. Now, if ever, was the occasion for dethroning them. After all, hadn't Mussolini thrown him out of Italy?

He agreed with most of this, and particularly with the idea that successive Governments of Great Britain had botched matters. "And yet I have warned them time and again," he added. There floated before me a picture of Aleister Crowley, the Beast, presiding over an attentive Prime Minister and Cabinet somewhere, if not in Downing Street, seeking guidance and enlightenment on the forthcoming convulsions of the Aeon.

A little later when I was actually in the Armed Forces and war was declared, I received a letter from Aleister enclosing a patriotic poem beginning, I remember, with the line:

> "Resistless as the gales that sweep".

The suggestion once again was that I should finance the publication of this and it stood to reason that vast profits would accrue to us both, and great stimulus to the war effort. In the letter he also suggested that we should correspond during the war. I suppose I replied to this, but I believe I never afterwards saw or wrote to him again. The next time I heard of him was to read of his death in 1947.

I understand that his last words were "I am perplexed." So am I.

# Crowley and the Press

Crowley's relations with the press were, on the whole, atrocious. Rather like *The Sun* and *News Of The World* today, with their revelations about pop stars, drug abusers, actresses, topless models and MPs, in Crowley's day publications such as *John Bull* and the *Sunday Express* delighted in freewheeling hyperbole if not actual libel. With his outrageous peregrinations and poses, The Great Beast 666 was one of their favourite targets.

Reproduced here are some actual pages of contemporary reports of Crowley's doings.

LONDON, THE SUNDAY EXPRESS, NOVE

## ALEISTER CROWLEY'S ORGIES IN SICILY.

### WOMAN'S ACCOUNT OF HIS LAST VISIT TO LONDON.

### "THE BEAST 666."

(CONTINUED FROM PAGE ONE.)

Association known as the A.A. (Atlantean Adepts), and later became a member of a Rosicrucian Society, known as the O.T.O. (Ordo Templi Orientis).

His adepts begin every letter and conversation with the greeting, "Do what thou wilt is the whole of the law" (evidently suggested by Rabelais' "Fay ce que voudrais"), and end up, "Love is the law, Love under will."

In 1910 Crowley was holding meetings at the Caxton Hall to witness the performance of the "Rites of Eleusis"; he cultivated an immoral society for the worship of the god Pan; and he organised every kind of evil rite including the "Cult of the Beetle" and the Black

the police authorities knew of his presence. He at once packed up and went. I understand that he stayed for a few nights at a Turkish bath establishment in the West End before leaving the country."

### BESTIAL ORGIES IN SICILY.

### CAKES OF GOATS' BLOOD AND HONEY.

The story of the bestial orgies conducted by Aleister Crowley in Sicily sounds like the ravings of a criminal lunatic, made mad by his own depravity, and was related yesterday to a "Sunday Express" representative by a woman who has just returned from this

2 of "THE LITTLE GARDEN"
...lightfully interesting little journal, full of invaluable
...nd suggestions for the amateur with only a small
...will be **GIVEN AWAY** with

# Sunday

TWOPENCE

**NO. 217.**

LONDON, F...

# NEW SINISTER REVELATIO...

## "AVAGING" IRISH...

### ...AVE FACTS TO BE FACED.

### ...RISH TROOPS OR ...HE FREE STATE?

### ...HE CHOICE.

...he "Sunday Express" Political
**Correspondent.**

...RE is an even greater
...agedy in Irish affairs than
...ul series of murders which
...ue to debase the name of
...en in the eyes of the world.

...most poignant and grave
...r is in the savaging of Irish
...hat is going on everywhere.
...s of fifteen are being taught
...to burn, to kill. They do it
...name of "The Republic,"
...which mean nothing more to
...mmature minds than a signal
...se the animal in themselves
...hrow off all restraints of
...ation.

### A CLEAR ISSUE.

...widespread is this process
...he decent men and women of
...d look with horror on the
...unless Law and Order win
...resent struggle.

...hen these boys are of age,"
...say, "we shall have a nation
...ated by savages who know no
...law than the gratification of
...worst instincts."

...other fact that is agitating
...ing men and women is the
...ble return of the British forces
...s the Free State Government

---

## "LI...

### CO-I...
### GERA...

"**Sunday E**...

WASHING...
The ex-Crown...
shortly make a...
the limelight of...
It is practically...
will be cited in t...

**MISS GERALDINE FARRAR.**

---

### Law Report, April 13

#### HIGH COURT OF JUSTICE
#### KING'S BENCH DIVISION

"BLACK MAGIC": LIBEL ACTION FAILS

CROWLEY v. CONSTABLE AND CO.,
LIMITED, AND OTHERS

*Before* Mr. JUSTICE SWIFT *and a Special Jury*

The jury stopped the case and returned a
verdict for the defendants in the action by
Mr. Edward Alexander (Aleister) Crowley, an
author, of Carlos Place, Grosvenor Square, W.,
against Constable and Co., Limited, of Orange
Street, W.C., Charles Wittingham and Griggs
(Printers), Limited, of Brunswick Park Road,
London, and Miss Nina Hamnett in respect of
an alleged libel in a book entitled "Laughing
Torso," published, printed, and written by the
defendants respectively.

Mr. Crowley complained that in "Laughing
Torso," Miss Hamnett stated that he had had a
temple at Cefalu, in Sicily, where he was supposed to have practised Black Magic.

The defendants denied that the words complained of were defamatory and further pleaded
that, if they were, they were true in substance
and in fact.

Mr. J. P. Eddy, Mr. Constantine Gallop, and
Mr. F. A. Lewis appeared for the plaintiff;
Mr. Malcolm Hilbery, K.C., and Mr. C. W.
Lilley for the publishers and printers of the
book; and Mr. Martin O'Connor for Miss
Hamnett. Mr. Arthur Reade held a watching
brief for an interested party.

Mrs. Betty Sedgwick, who visited Cefalu with
her former husband, "Raoul" Loveday, in
1922, and gave evidence on behalf of the defence
yesterday (Thursday), denied, in further cross-
examination, that, before her marriage, her life
might fairly be described as "drink, drugs, and
immorality."

Mr. EDDY.—Which part is inaccurate ?—I
have not drugged for years.

Drink ?—I consumed about the amount which
anybody else would.

Persistent immorality ?—No.

Living a very fast life in London ?—No.

When you married your husband was he in a
poor state of health ?—He had been very ill six
months previously, but he was getting quite fit.

Did you try to involve him in the life which
you were living in London ?—I was a model
and I had to keep both of us, so how could I do
that ? We had no money and I had to work
every day.

Mr. EDDY said that he suggested that Mrs.
Sedgwick was " the source of all these stories
about the ' Worst Man in the World ' and
' orgies ' in Sicily. Mrs. Sedgwick agreed that
she had given information about Cefalu to a
...nday newspaper. The article which was pub-
...owever, did not accurately reproduce the
...had given.

...ared that her story that a
...of the ceremonies

---

## ...ORD BEAVERBROOK ...FOR PALESTINE.

...OMPANIED BY MR.
JAMES DOUGLAS.

Beaverbrook and Mr. James
...ave left London for Palestine,
...which is partially in the nature
...y, will be broken by easy
Mr. Douglas, who always sees
...gh the eyes of an individualist
...nticist, will contribute a
...of his impressions and de-
... "Sunday Express."

---

## ...N CAPTAIN
...INSANE.

...S TRAINED ON
...'S PALACE.

...Correspondent.
...NOPLE.
...rday, Feb. 24.
...which caused a
...oreign warships
...is week have
...cruiser sud-
...guns in his
...ned on the
...otche. The
...with the
...l the facts
...Shall we

...he Iron
...done.
...to be
...his

---

## 'VAR...

### ENTI...
### "...

### DREAD
### OF

### CROW...

THE reve...
Expres...
orgies ca...
Crowley—...
styles hims...
Cefalu, Sic...
by a sinist...

Informati...
newspaper...
One of th...
English ur...
is dead.

His young...
minent in L...
in London t...
collapse. S...
than a hint...
she has esc...

### WORSE

She said,...
press" repre...
story of...
debauches a...
in this new...
real horror...
at Cefalu, w...
practises his...

This young...
of her husba...
withholds ir...
sorrow, said...
husband a s...
when in Lon...
of a persuas...
The young c...
character of...
inviting the...

# Express

## LATE LONDON EDITION

...ARY 25, 1923.

TWOPENCE.

# S OF ALEISTER CROWLEY

## ...Y LAD'S DEATH.

### ...O TO ...Y"

#### ...ORDEAL ...OUNG

#### ...PLANS.

...the "Sunday ...ly of obscene ...by Aleister ...st 666," as he ...s "abbey" at ...been followed ...gic happening. ...st reached this ...latest victims. ...rilliant young ...man, a writer,

...eautiful girl pro... ...c circles, arrived ...go in a state of ...le to give more ...rors from which

#### ...RS STILL.

...a "Sunday Ex... ...esterday that the ...rowley's sexual ...gies as published ...understates the ...in the "abbey" ...s his women and ...se. ...name and that ...unday Express" ...to the parents" ...wley offered her ...ost last autumn ...east is possess... ...suave manner... ...idea of the t... ...to which he t... ...offer seem...

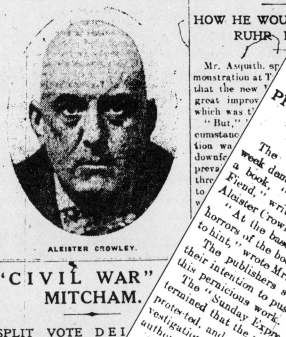

**ALEISTER CROWLEY.**

## "CIVIL WAR" MITCHAM.

### SPLIT VOTE DE... TORIES' OPPON...

Sir A. Griffith Bosca...
Mr. J. T. Catterall...
Mr. H. E. Brown...
Mr. J. Ede (Lab...

(Polling ...

There is no w...
The rival Tor...
are far more...
than against...
ing parties...
The B...
nouncing...
eleven...
teral"...
is a...
sl...

## "I AM NOT AF... OF LABOU...

### HOW HE WOULD ... RUHR PR...

Mr. Asquath, sp...
monstration at T...
that the new...
great improv...
which was t...
"But,"...
cumstance...
tion wa...
downfa...
preva...
thre...
to...
w...

## BLACK RECORD OF ALEISTER CROWLEY.

### PREYING ON THE DEBASED.

#### HIS ABBEY.

### PROFLIGACY AND VICE IN SICILY.

The "Sunday Express" last week demanded the suppression of a book, "The Diary of a Drug Fiend," written by a person called Aleister Crowley.

"At the baser and more bestial horrors of the book it is impossible to hint," wrote Mr. James Douglas.

The publishers state that it is their intention to push the sales of this pernicious work.

The "Sunday Express" was determined that the public should be protected, and made the fullest investigations into the career of the author.

**These investigations have produced the most astounding revelations.**

The man Aleister Crowley is the organiser of societies for pagan orgies.

He engaged in pro-German propaganda during the war.

He published obscene attacks on the King.

He made a dramatic renunciation of his British birthright.

He proclaimed himself "King of Ireland."

He stole money from a woman.

He now conducts an "Abbey" in Sicily.

**He was in London a month a... unknown to any one exc... small circle of intim...**

This is the ma... work is a delib... obscenity... cency...

## ...ASPHEMO... ...CTURE ...TION ... ...B...

### ...Corre... ...ORK, S... ...Feb. 24

...ON has be... ...y a remarka... ...ed at the Wa... ...ich represents ... ...tionists—Mr. W... ...gressman Volstea... ..."Volstead" law, an... ...Anderson, director of ... ...loon League—interru... ...arriage at Cana, in Gali... ...Christ turned water into...

The painter places Ch... ...rounded by protesting ... ...guests, in the foregrou... ...Bryan is kneeling on ... ...emptying jugs of the liq... ...by Christ's miracle con... ...verted from water into...

Mr. Volstead, with his ... ...Christ's shoulder, is p... ...protest to other jugs ... ...wine, while Mr. Anderson ...ing with dilated eyes M... ...defiance of the Divine an...

A prohibition officer ... ...occupies a doorway in ... ...ground.

The painter is Mr. J ... ...Kaufman, and the pict... ...part of the annual exhibi... ...Society of Independent

...e proposition ...e should hold ...cy of cowardice ...tion, which does ...traditions and ...It is more clear ...at you should first ...ation of the United ...the authority of the

## SEIZED IN ...HE RUHR.

## RACE GANG ...

ATTEMPT TO BRI... OFFICIALS ?

An alleged attempt to ...

...ONALISTS ORGANISING FOR A RISING.

# A Beastly Poet?

*Opposite*: 'The Beast' at large: Crowley in the Satanic, bald-headed pose beloved of the Fleet Street hacks. Mad, bad and dangerous to know!

While we may not agree with Crowley's own estimation of himself as 'England's greatest poet', we need not plunge to the other extreme of Yeats's grudging admission that he perhaps penned one or two lines of real poetry and no more. He was, after all, included in the *Oxford Book Of Mystical Verse* as well as Heffer's *Cambridge Poets 1900–13* anthology.

The first four poems here are from the unpublished *Book Of Oaths*, and have only previously been seen in Alan Burnett-Rae's *Memoir Of 666* limited-edition booklet.

## HYMN TO TERMINUS

Terminus! so colossal calm
Thy face, so square thy pedestal.
Is it to Thee I speak my Psalm,
Give Thee the final praise of all?
Was all the rest ephemeral?

Is it before Thy shrine that man
Is given at last to comprehend
The mocking riddle, the blank plan
Of Life? Seest Thou all things intend
To some intelligible End?

All Gods adore Thee, Thou the sum
Of their vast ledgers, the effect
Of infinite causes that were dumb
To soul-search as to intellect,
So let mine agony expect!

For in me there's a spirit obscene
That sneers and jeers: "Fantastic fool!
What end of aught, clean or unclean,
Hast Thou beheld or known? What rule
Stands first of all thought's penal school?

"Doth winter end the year, or day
End night? Is some effect thou knowest
That is not also Cause? The Way
of Nature is the Snake's. Thou goest.
All go, the highest and the lowest".

Term ends; the goal we panted after
Despite the dust proves one mark
Of myriads – hear the ironic laughter
(Self-aimed!) Of those who watch us bark
Shins as we stumble in the dark.

Infinite Space and Time to explore
As the God waltzes with the Germ!
All man can do – and God no more! –
Is rhythm faultless and feet firm,
To dance his way from Term to Term.

I am not weary, Terminus!
I am game to take all chances, spend
Myself, stern, slack, suave, strenuous
As may be – or to call Thee friend,
If, after all, Thou be the End!

## THE LIZARD

One does not need to be a wizard,
To meddle with forbidden arts;
In order that the lively lizard
May teach us (lay it to your hearts)
Some pithy points – I think he can
Assist the busy business man.

The lizard is alert, suspicious;
He twists and turns with subtle speed;
He is not stubborn or malicious,
He never fights unless he need;
And if you grab him, you will find
He bolts, and leaves his tail behind.

I need not even be at pains
To shew the drift of these instructions.
The very simplest business brains
Are capable of such deductions.
I echoed the sighed thought "It *is* hard
I wasn't born to be a lizard!"

## INSIDE INFORMATION

I am assured that every man is God
Because the simplest-minded, dullest youth
Witless and ignorant, a stock, a clod,
Has perfect understanding of Pure Truth.

Innate, exact, identical with mine,
Though all in vain Philosophy has sweated
That simplest concept even to define
Humanity is certainly indebted.

To intellect for divers useful arts;
But when it comes to any serious odds,
Our brains play second fiddle to our hearts –
Damned lucky that we happen to be Gods!

## CRADLE SONG

Slumber, my soul, a little while
The butterfly may fold its wings.
Soften thy silence with a smile,
But brood not on the truth of things!

"A little while!" What words to thee,
Thou ended never or begun!
To thee, to sleep is not to be.
To be and not to be are one.

Or was it that thy dreams create
These wheels of mystery that revolve
Under the force of Chance or Fate?
– And at thy waking they dissolve.

My soul, thou hast not wit nor care
If all exist, if all that shews
Be, how things came or how they fare,
If all the riot be repose.

Thou art in all, no soul apart,
And all in thee eternal springs;
Nothing can save that thou art,
Naught more save Light-waves of thy wings.

Thou sleep? 'Tis mind that sleeps or dies.
I? But a tear thou has loved to weep!
It wearies me to be so wise –
Watch thou! I turn my face to sleep.

## HYMN TO LUCIFER

Ware, nor of good nor ill, what aim hath act?
Without its climax, death, what savour hath
Life? an impeccable machine, exact
He paces an inane and pointless path
To glut brute appetites, his sole content
How tedious were he fit to comprehend
Himself! More, this our noble element
Of fire in nature, love in spirit, unkenned
Life hath no spring, no axle, and no end.

His body a blood-ruby radiant
With noble passion, sun-souled Lucifer
Swept through the dawn colossal, swift aslant
On Eden's imbecile perimeter.
He blessed nonentity with every curse
And spiced with sorrow the dull soul of sense,
Breathed life into the sterile universe,
With Love and Knowledge drove out innocence
The Key of Joy is disobedience.

Crowley's *Hymn To Lucifer*, rarely seen in
print but often commented upon by those
who haven't read it!

The following poems, previously unpublished,
show the range of Crowley's poetic style:
from the erotic to the spiritual to the
downright silly.

## THE RED LIPS OF THE OCTOPUS

The red lips of the octopus
Are more than myriad stars of night.
The great beast writhes in furier form than thirty stallions amorous!
I would they clung to me and stung! would they quenched me with delight.
The red lips of the octopus.

They reek with poison of the sea
Silent and hot and langourous
My skin drinks in their slaver warm, my sweat his wrapt embrace excite
The heavy sea rolls languidly over the ensanguined kiss of us
We strain and strive, we die for love. We linger in the lusty fight
We agonize; our clutch becomes more cruel and murderous.
My passion splashes out at last. Ah! with what ecstasy I bite
The red lips of the octopus.

## THE END – RONDEL (1896)

The end of everything – the veil of night
Is not so deep I cannot comprehend
I see before me yawn – a ghastly sight –
The End.

Love long ago deserted me to wend
His way with younger men. Life spreads a blight
Over men now. I have not one friend.

There is no hope for me; no gleam of light
In my black path will any comfort lend –
Yet will I meet with smiling face, upright
The End

## G-R-R-R-R! (1916)

Oh cabbage-heads soaked in rum!
On the blink, on the tum!
It's right, tight, put out the light!
Putty faces!
Oh grimaces
At this time of night!
Let me draw, paint, sculp
Your faces of pulp!
Oh gulp!
Put out the light!
Diabolically, divinely bright tight!

What do you know about that?
I'm a cat!
The world's my rat!
It all goes under my hat
Thin and fat,
Oh my mat,
I'll paint
You all, like a saint,
Until I faint
Ain't
That quaint?
Gr-r-r-r!
Gr-r-r-r-r-r!
Once more for luck
(Love a duck)
Gr-r-r-r-r-r-r-r-r-r!

# The Masks
# of The Beast

*Opposite*: **The English Gent**. This was a look that Crowley always enjoyed, loving as he did the idea of playing the upper-crust snob. But in the 1920's he wrote, 'I have been faithless in many ways: I have tried in particular to combine my mission with living the regular life of an English Gentleman. And the gods won't allow it. They have checkmated my plans with ever-increasing severity.'

*Right*: **Mahatma Guru Sri Paramahansa Shivaji**. One of Aleister Crowley's oriental aliases, adopted primarily for his authorship of the masterwork *Eight Lectures on Yoga*.

Crowley never lost his childlike love of fancy-dress and make-believe. Sometimes the costumes and bizarre pseudonyms were of real occult significance, but more often than not he simply indulged in exoticism for its own sake.

The following are just some of the masks of the master over the years.

*Above*: **Prince Chioa Khan**. On honeymoon in Cairo with his first wife, Rose, Crowley suddenly adopted this impressive name for no good reason other than that he wanted to pose in cloth-of-gold coat, silken jacket, luxuriant beard and so forth.

*Above right*: **Osiris Risen**. Crowley in 1899, formulating the Pentagram in a ritual during the early stages of his magical awakening.

*Left*: **Baphomet, the Supreme and Holy King of Ireland, Iona, and all the Britains that are in the Sanctuary of the Gnosis**. Here Crowley is wearing his Masonic regalia as head of the OTO for Britain in 1916.

*Below*: **The Mad Arab**. Crowley smoking his favourite mixture, rum-soaked perique tobacco, while dressed in Arabian costume.

# Crapulous Contemporaries?

The Hermetic Order Of The Golden Dawn, that legendary organisation which gave Crowley his first real taste of magical ritual and romance, still exerts a powerful influence on the occultists of today. The documents on which it is originally based may well have been forgeries, it may have ended its days fragmented and in utter disarray, the style of its magick may seem outmoded to modern practitioners of the art, and yet the vast number of books still being published about the Golden Dawn attests to a lingering authority, albeit hotly contested by newer cults.

Perhaps the aura of power connected with the Golden Dawn has something to do with the quality of its members over the years. Crowley may not have thought much of those he encountered, but history has judged differently. Here is a small selection of the Golden Dawn's more notable adepts or members.

**William Butler Yeats** The great Irish poet was very active in the affairs of the Golden Dawn, especially in the dispute with Mathers and Crowley, and its aftermath. His magical and mystical interests are inextricably woven into much of his verse. He is said to have bored Aubrey Beardsley stiff with his constant prating about 'dyah-bolism'.

Magical motto: *Demon Est Deus Inversus* (the Devil is the converse of God).

**Arthur Edward Waite** Guiding-light behind the most popular modern Tarot deck, Waite was a prolific author whose influence can be seen in the work of his disciples, such as Charles Williams and Evelyn Underhill. He collaborated with Arthur Machen and his career as a writer lasted almost until the Second World War. Although Crowley went on to slate his

*Left*: Arthur Machen, the weird genius of Caerlon-On-Usk and the subject of a revival of interest at the moment.

*Opposite*: Algernon Blackwood, master of the atmospheric ghost story.

dull, verbose and somewhat deliberately obscure style ('Wisdom While You Waite', went one lampoon), it was Waite's *Book Of Black Magic And Of Pacts* that initially put Crowley on the occult trail.

Magical motto: *Sacramentum Regis* (the Sacrament of the King).

**Florence Farr** Named, it's thought, by her father in honour of his friend Florence Nightingale, Florence was the ideal 'new woman'. She turned her hand to anything she fancied (in-

cluding men; she had had 14 lovers by the time she was in her early 30s). She became a celebrated actress and was much admired by Yeats as well as George Bernard Shaw and was also the author of a famous book called *Egyptian Magic* which is still available today.

Magical motto: *Sapientia Sapienti Dono Data* (Wisdom is given to the wise as a gift).

**Arthur Machen** There is something of a contemporary revival of Machen's writing, with modern writers of horror tales praising his

strange little stories of elemental evil, the most notable of which is *The Great God Pan*.

Inspired by a magical boyhood in Caerlon-On-Usk in Wales, Machen was always in love with the idea of powers beyond human ken and was a favourite author of the American master of the macabre, H P Lovecraft. Famed for his tale of ancient ghosts helping the British during the First World War battle of Mons, *The Bowmen* (which was taken for fact by many), Machen seems to have been a relatively low-key Golden Dawn member.

Magical motto: *Avallaunius* (from *The Gar-den of Avallaunius*, the original title of his masterpiece, *The Hill of Dreams*).

**Algernon Blackwood** Creator of occult detective John Silence and author of many classic horror tales including *The Willows*, this prolific author broadcast in later years for the BBC and became known as 'the Ghost Man' by his fans.

Magical motto: *Umbram Fugat Veritas* (Shadows flee the truth.)

*Note*: This list is simply a small selection of Golden Dawn members who became famous in

*Opposite*: Sax Rohmer, creator of Dr Fu-Manchu and always fascinated by the occult. His book, *The Romance of Sorcery*, is still a minor classic of magickal history.

*Right*: Bram Stoker, author of *Dracula* (1897) and student of the macabre.

other walks of life. Any list based on importance relating to the Golden Dawn itself could hardly omit Mathers, Annie Horniman, Westcott, Felkin, Ayton, Gardner *et al*.

Two other famous writers, both alleged Golden Dawn alumni, cannot go unmentioned: Bram Stoker, manager of Sir Henry Irving and author of *Dracula*, has often been spoken of as a member, but no real evidence for this exists. In studying Stoker's career it's hard to see where he could have found the time for occult activities between full-time work at Irving's Lyceum and writing his many books. Also, Sax Rohmer

(Arthur Sarsfield Ward), creator of Fu-Manchu, while doubtless a serious student of the occult despite the active opposition of his wife, seems not to have been a bona fide Golden Dawn member. *Master of Villainy*, an excellent biography by his widow and his disciple, is on shaky ground when it asserts that Rohmer was a Golden Dawn adept and an enemy of Crowley without giving any details or proof. While the latter is possible the former appears as dubious as the book's story that Rohmer was also in a Rosicrucian Society (dating from the 16th century) along with Rudyard Kipling!

# Crowley's Wit

Aleister Crowley is hardly well-known as a wit, and yet dubious limericks, cruel satires and odd tales dropped glibly from his lips at the slightest opportunity. This item originally appeared in the now-defunct magazine *Lilliput*, and illustrates that Crowley could have made a living out of spinning anecdotes to *Reader's Digest*-type publications had he not had his mind on higher (and lower) things.

### How To Tell An Englishman From An American

This is the funniest story in the world. I first came across it in the Green-room Club. Beerbohm Tree was present; also Nat Goodwin. He offered the following:

In a small town of the remoter districts of the Middle West a young man was standing, shuffling his feet on the sidewalk. Presently he saw coming towards him a stranger – a God-fearing, clean-living He-man, a hundred per cent. American. This man he stopped, and said, "Excuse me, Stranger, but can you tell me the way to the Post Office?" "Yes," said the other, and walked on. But he had not gone fifty yards before his heart smote him, and he said to himself: "I allow that was pretty smart of me just now; but was it Christ-like? Was it Service? I dare say that young man is a God-fearing, clean-living He-man, a hundred per cent. American, just the way I am myself, and I dare say he has not had a letter from the old folks in their lonely cottage for a long, long time, and he has tramped all the way in from the farm where he is working in the hopes of a letter – and I have to be rude to him! No Sir! The least I can do is to go back and put him right."

So he went back to the young man, who was still shuffling his feet on the sidewalk, and said to him: "Say, brother, I guess I was rude to you just now. You want to know the way to the Post Office, don't you?" "No," said the young man, and walked on. That is the story.

There were some Americans in the Club; they all laughed, but none of the English moved a muscle. At last, however, somebody asked Tree point-blank whether *he* saw anything funny in the story, and Tree, after due consideration, could do no more than pronounce in his inimitable drawl: "I think they were both damned rude."

*Below*: Little left but pipe and wit? A rare picture of Aleister Crowley.

*Right*: One fat
Englishman?
Crowley in a
Churchillian pose.

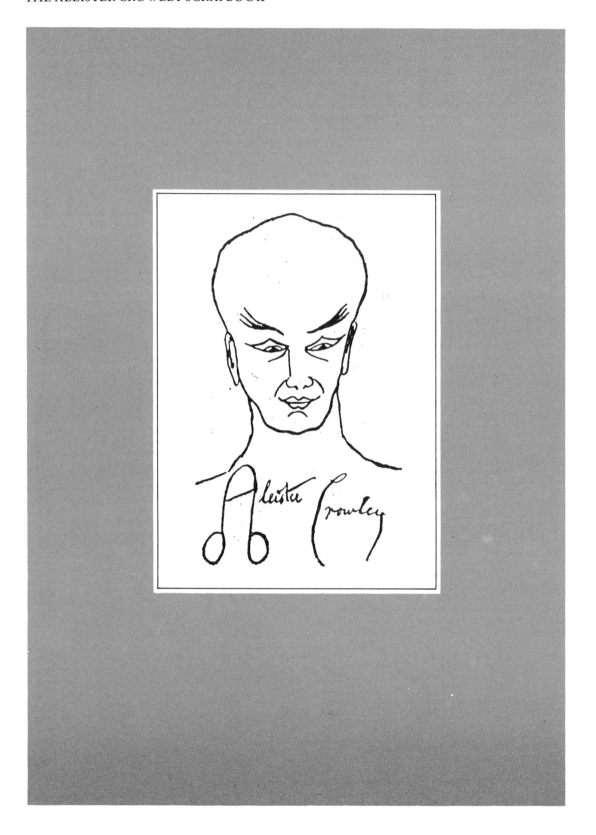

# The Filth
# and the Fury

*Opposite*:
Self-portrait with his
usual phallic-style
signature.

One wonders whether Crowley ever regretted his erotic
outpourings. Books such as *White Stains* (1898), *Snowdrops
From A Curate's Garden* (1904), *The Bagh-I-Muattar* (1910)
and the slightly less vile *Clouds Without Water* (1909) kept
cropping up throughout his life at the most inconvenient
moments – indeed, some of the poems would still deeply
shock many people today. *White Stains*, in fact, cost Crowley
his lawsuit against Nina Hamnett: 'I have no hesitation,' his
lawyer told him, 'in saying that if the Defendants are in
possession of that book your chances of winning this action
are negligible. I can see no satisfactory explanation of it.'

Although it seems that most copies of his limited-editions
of these hard-core pornographic efforts were destroyed, at
one time or another, by H.M. Customs, reprints are now
available from specialist shops for those with stomachs
strong enough to stand graphic lust, necrophilia, coprophilia,
sodomy, cruelty and so on. It's unfortunately impossible to
print an example of Crowley's sexually-frantic work in a
mainstream book like the present volume: no distributor
would handle such stuff, I'm assured. We can, however, take
a chance on reprinting the Beast's gloriously raunchy signature, which appears on the opposite page.

*Below, left*: Another,
less obvious, piece of
penile symbolism by
Aleister Crowley.

*Below, right*: The seal
of the A∴A∴,
Crowley's magickal
organisation.

*Dear Poet,*
 *Please send me.... cop.... of this at once. I enclose the cash.*
 *Yours truly,*

To A. CROWLEY. *Boleskine. Foyers. Inverness.*

# WHY

# JESUS

Special edition, of 100 copies only, privately printed on handmade paper, is now offered at Two Guineas net to subscribers.

# WEPT by Aleister Crowley

Who has now ceased to weep.

*With* the original Dedications !

*With* the advertisement which has brought Peace and Joy to so many a sad heart !!

*With* the slip containing the solution of the difficulty on pages 75-76 !!!

*With* the improper joke on page 38 !!!!

*With* the beetle-crushing retort to M$^r$ G. K. Chesterton's aborted attack upon the Sword of Song !!!!!

*With* the specially contributed Appeal from the Poet's Mamma !!!!!!

Look slippy, boys ! Christ may come at any moment. He won't like it if you haven't read the book about His melt.

Unique opportunity. — Order early to avoid Armageddon!

# Why Jesus Wept. by ALEISTER CROWLEY

(who weeps too).

A study of Society and of the Grace of God.

Limited edition at £ 1-1-0 uniform with the "Sword of Song," but in black throughout.

---

Mr Aleister Crowley solicits subscriptions for the above remarkable investigation (in dramatic form) into a critical point of the Religious History of the West. Apply to the Hon. Sec., S.P.R.T., Boleskine, Foyers, Inverness, N.B.

---

Are you a young and tender-hearted maiden? W. J. W. will delight you, and fill you with beautiful thought.

Are you a devout Mystic? In W. J. W. is the key to Beatitude.

Are you a hustling business man? W. J. W. will tone up your harried nervous system.

Are you a poet? W. J. W. will not cut your hair; but it will raise it.

Are you a dog-fancier? You will never beat the breed of bitches in W. J. W.

Are you a theologian? W. J. W. proves that Christ was no lachrymose hysterical hypochondriac, but a man with a genuine grievance.

Are you a Christian? W. J. W. tells how God's Grace can destroy the Works of the Devil.

W. J. W. touches Society with a needle; Religion with a pitchfork.

W. J. W. startles the Belle. W. J. W. annihilates the Quack.

Imposture cannot live in the breezy atmosphere of W. J. W.

Children love its dainty fooling: wise men pore over its profound revelations of the human heart.

The *Milwaukee Christian Science Tomahawk* says: "Now we know why."

The Catholic Press is unanimous in its favour. The *Society Snippet* says: "we recognise under the smiling mask of Angela the sinister and berouged features of Lady S. . . ."

*God's Gore*; with which is incorporated *Ghostly Goings-on; a paper for Godly Gaffers*, says: "The Blessed Blood again blots out Beelzebub's blasted blow-fly-blears."

I say: Buy! Buy Now! Quick! Quick!

My Unborn Child screams "Buy!"

These two Order Forms, for Crowley's 1904 book *Why Jesus Wept*, clearly show that the Beast was ahead of his time as a publicist. Considered horribly irreverent in their day, these flyers would not look out-of-place publicising an outrageous rock group today. They would probably fit equally well into the back pages of a current issue of *Private Eye*.

# The Art of a Master

*Opposite*: Leah Hirsig, Crowley's 'Scarlet Woman', in his studio with a portrait of herself as a 'dead soul'.

*Below*: 'The Waste Land,' Crowley's sketch of an astral landscape.

Crowley dabbled with painting and sketching throughout the latter part of his life; his art – like all that he did – being an expression of his magickal ideas. He may have been an indifferent draughtsman, but what his pictures lack technically they make up for in crude power.

'Each painting reveals an unknown part of me to myself,' he wrote. 'I gain real knowledge through my art. Is not that better fun than if it merely recorded my thought with mechanical precision?'

Aleister Crowley went so far as to declare the Impressionist artist Paul Gauguin a saint, seeing a parallel between

himself and the artist in the fact that they both liked to daub the walls of their dwellings! Doubtless, however, Crowley's most impressive display of his artistic nature was when he apparently returned from the dead in 1930 (he had faked suicide by leaving some clothes on a beach, pre-empting British politician John Stonehouse and comedy series hero Reginald Perrin by half a century) to open his one-man show at Berlin's PORZA Galleries, where one of those immortalised in pen-and-ink was Aldous Huxley.

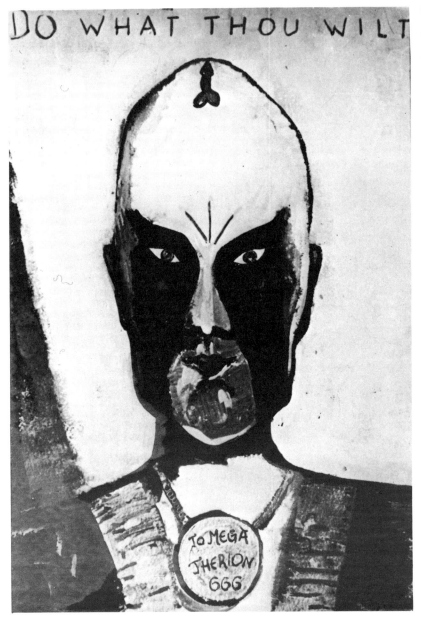

*Above*: A surprisingly accomplished pen-and-ink drawing of Satan by Crowley. The picture was recently bought by a Canadian collector.

*Left*: Crowley by Crowley. Note the phallic forelock!

*Opposite*: A Crowley sketch of the demon Choronzon at lunch.

*Above*: Sketch by
Crowley of his
second wife, Maria de
Miramar.

*Above*: A hitherto unpublished oil painting by
Aleister Crowley, possibly depicting (on the
right) Leah, his Scarlet Woman. It remains in
a private collection.

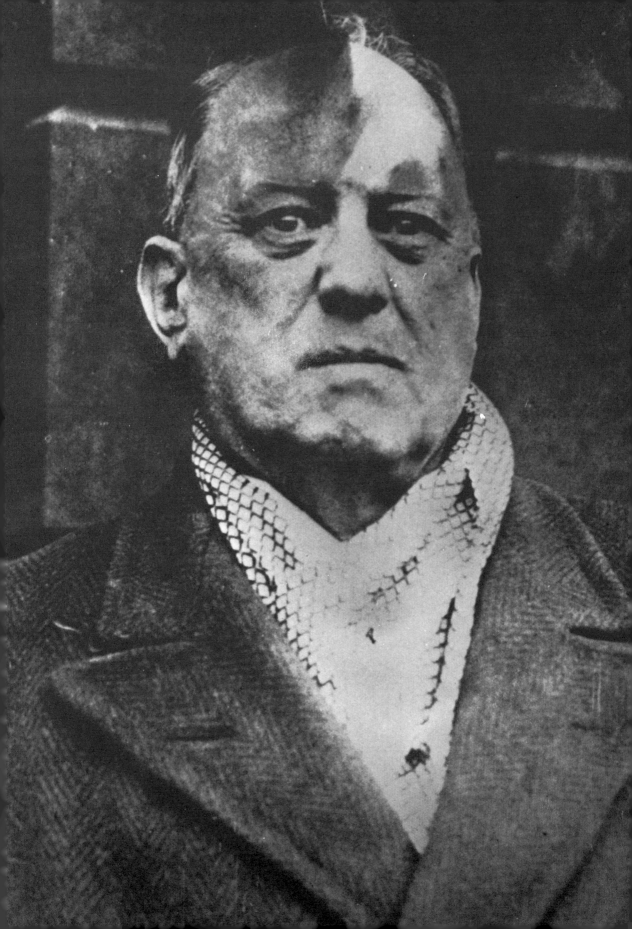

# A Scandal in Bohemia

One of the scarcest Crowleyan items seems to be *The Rosicrucian Scandal*, published under the agreeably silly and pompous pseudonym of 'Leo Vincey' in 1911. A fairly incomprehensible item, it nevertheless oozes with Crowley's vitriolic sarcasm, directed at his ex-Master Mathers. It involves a vicious lampoon of the evidence Mathers had given the previous year in trying to prevent the continuing publication of Golden Dawn secrets in Crowley's *Equinox* magazine.

The 'Mrs Horos' referred to in the pamphlet was an unpleasant character who had, with her husband, run a fake Golden Dawn. Their motive was that most common spur: power, money, sex. Although they convinced many for a short time (Mathers included) they drew hefty jail sentences in 1901 for their corrupt practices.

While *The Rosicrucian Scandal* may puzzle newcomers to the Crowley canon, its reappearance here after years of obscurity will delight the serious collector.

THE

## "Rosicrucian" Scandal

by

LEO VINCEY

# THE "ROSICRUCIAN" SCANDAL

Mr. Aleister Crowley, Editor of *"The Equinox,"* having published the facts concerning the "Rosicrucians" in various numbers of that magazine, has been attacked by the gang whom he exposed in such a way that he has had no opportunity to make clear the facts in a more public manner.

Mr. Crowley is debarred from taking legal action by the reasons set forth hereafter. I have therefore determined to publish in a striking form the truth of the matter, less to defend him (he has no need of it) than to bring to an end the villanies of the "Rosicrucian" gang.

I have proceeded on the principle that Mathers is obliged either to tell the truth or to repeat his previous statements. The latter are indicated by inverted commas.

It is against the express wish of Mr. Crowley that I have, in his own phrase, "played scavenger"; but I rather break my Vow of Holy Obedience than allow his work to be hindered, as I cannot but maintain that it has been hindered hitherto.

LEO VINCEY

## SUMMARY OF PERSONS REFERRED TO IN THE DIALOGUE

MATHERS ........................ *Self-appointed "Head" of the*
4. Rue de la Source, aux *"Rosicrucian Order."*
Gressets, par La Celle-
Saint-Cloud.

CRAN ............................... *Perjured shyster.\**
5. King's Bench Walk
Temple, W.C.

BERRIDGE ......................... *Homœopathic doctor, etc.*

W. F. DE WEND FENTON ... *Editor of "The Looking-Glass." Turf trickster until warned off; since professional blackmailer to the nobility and gentry.*

DR. WYNN WESTCOTT ..... *Coroner, sorcerer, etc. Dupe and victim of*
396, Camden Road, N. *Mathers.*

ALEISTER CROWLEY ........ *Ex-dupe and victim of Mathers.*

(\*) Details of Cran's perjury in the Court of King's Bench in April, 1911 are here omitted for reasons which may become clear hereafter.

The Cross-Examination of Samuel Sidney Sylvester Scherzerade Socrates Scipio Schiller Simmons Scrutton Shacaback Swank

Swizzle Liddell Diddell Macgregor Mac Kerrow Mathers, James IV of Scotland, Comte de St. Germain, Earl of Glenstrae, Comte Macgregor, Chevalier Mac-gregor, Macgregor-Mathers, S'Rhiogail mo Dhream, Deo Duce Comite Ferro, Chevalier of the Order of St. Germain, etc., etc., by Mr. Q. Scorpio, one of His Majesty's Counsel learned in the Law.

SCORPIO, K.C. What is you name?

MATHERS. The whole lot?

SCORPIO, K.C. The name on your birth certificate.

MATHERS. Mathers.

SCORPIO, K.C. You were educated at Bedford Grammar School?

MATHERS. Yes.

SCORPIO, K.C. And became a lieutenant in a Hampshire volunteer regiment?

MATHERS. Yes.

SCORPIO, K.C. Yet in Paris you were engaged in Jacobite conspiracies to overthrow the throne of England?

MATHERS. I pretended to be.

SCORPIO, K.C. Were you actually so engaged?

MATHERS. I refuse to answer the question.

SCORPIO, K.C. You became a Rosicrucian?

MATHERS. "Yes."

SCORPIO, K.C. You hold high rank in the Order?

MATHERS. "I am the Head of the Rosicrucian Order."

SCORPIO, K.C. You have read the constitutions of that Order?

MATHERS. "Yes."

SCORPIO, K.C. It is a secret Order?

MATHERS. Yes.

SCORPIO, K.C. By the constitution no member is permitted to declare himself to be a member?

MATHERS. That is what Waite says.

SCORPIO, K.C. Who is Waite?

MATHERS. The greatest living authority on the Rosicrucians.

SCORPIO, K.C. Let me read what he says. "Let me warn my readers that all persons professing to be Rosicrucians are simply members of psuedo-fraternities, and that there is that difference between their assertion and the facts of the case in which the essence of a lie consists." What have you to say to that?

MATHERS. "I am the Head of the Rosicrucian Order."

SCORPIO, K.C. You are however responsible to secret chiefs?

MATHERS. "Yes."

SCORPIO, K.C. Who are they?

MATHERS. "I am sworn not to divulge them."

SCORPIO, K.C. In the constitutions of the Golden Dawn a Fräulein Sprengel or Sapiens Dominabitur Astris is named as one of them?

MATHERS. I suppose so.

SCORPIO, K.C. Is it so or not?

MATHERS. Yes.

SCORPIO, K.C.   In your letter to Mrs. Emery of the 16th Feby., 1900, you say: "It may interest you to know that Soror Sapiens Dominabitur Astris is now in Paris working with me"?

MATHERS.   Yes.

SCORPIO, K.C.   Was this Fräulein Sprengel?

MATHERS.   No.

SCORPIO, K.C.   Who was it?

MATHERS.   Madame Horos, better known, perhaps, as "the Swami."

SCORPIO, K.C.   The same Madame Horos who in 1901 received a sentence of seven years' penal servitude for abominable offences against children?

MATHERS.   How was I to know that she would be found out?

SCORPIO, K.C.   You acknowledged her as your spiritual superior?

MATHERS.   Yes.

SCORPIO, K.C.   As a secret chief $8° = 3°$?

MATHERS.   Yes.

SCORPIO, K.C.   Thank you. Now with regard to Allan Bennett. He was staying with you in Paris.?

MATHERS.   Yes.

SCORPIO, K.C.   How employed?

MATHERS.   In trying to make rubies from ruby dust.

SCORPIO, K.C.   Did he succeed?

MATHERS.   He made a small worthless ruby.

SCORPIO, K.C.   With better apparatus he might have made a commercial success of the process?

MATHERS.   I cannot say.

SCORPIO, K.C.   In point of fact, a precisely similar process is being worked at this day with success?

MATHERS.   Yes.

SCORPIO, K.C.   What was his moral character in regard to sexual matters?

MATHERS.   He had an aversion to all such matters amounting to horror.

SCORPIO, K.C.   What was the condition of his health?

MATHERS.   He was a constant sufferer from spasmodic asthma in its most aggravated form.

SCORPIO, K.C.   He took drugs habitually?

MATHERS.   Yes, by the orders of his doctor.

SCORPIO, K.C.   Never for pleasure?

MATHERS.   Never.

SCORPIO, K.C.   How can you be sure?

MATHERS.   When he left England, the change of climate cured at least temporarily his disease, and he instantly abandoned the practice.

SCORPIO, K.C.   He left you on good terms?

MATHERS.   Yes.

SCORPIO, K.C.   And you have never quarrelled with him since?

MATHERS.   Never.

SCORPIO, K.C.   Then why do you defame him now and allow the vilest crimes to be imputed to him?

MATHERS.   Anything to damage Crowley!

SCORPIO, K.C.   Did you quarrel with him ever at the time?

MATHERS.   Yes.

SCORPIO, K.C.   Let me read you the published account of your quarrel:

> He (Crowley) had, as we have seen, induced Mathers to put in force the Deadly and Hostile Current of Will but, as in the case of the Jackdaw of Rheims, nobody seemed a penny the worse. One might have expected that Mathers having failed, Aleister Crowley would have abandoned him. No, for it seemed still possible that Mathers, really in touch with the Supreme Chiefs, had yet finally decided to say with Christ upon the Cross: "Father, forgive them, for they know not what they do," even though this theory was somewhat rudely shaken by Mathers spending the whole of one Sunday afternoon in rattling a lot of dried peas in a sieve under the impression that they were the revolted members: as subsequent events proved, they were only the ideas in his head. So we find Aleister Crowley still loyal, if a little sceptical, and searching within himself to discover a touchstone by which he might prove beyond doubt the authenticity of Mathers' claim to represent the Masters. Now, there had been a good deal of talk of an adventure that happened to Mathers and Allan Bennett, who was guest in his house, in which a revolver figured prominently; but the story was only vague, and Allan Bennett, who could and would have, told the truth about it, had departed for a distant colony. So on arriving in Paris, Aleister Crowley lured Mathers into telling the story, which was as follows: That he and Allan Bennett had disagreed upon an obscure point in theology, thereby formulating the accursed Dyad, thereby enabling the Abramelin demons to assume material form: one in his own shape, another in that of Allan Bennett. Now, the demon that looked like Allan Bennett had a revolver, and threatened to shoot him (Mathers), while the demon that resembled himself was equally anxious to shoot Allan Bennett. Fortunately, before the demons could fire, Mrs. Mathers came into the room, thus formulating the symbol of the blessed Trinity, of which her great purity of character would naturally fit her to be a prominent member. Now, the only probability about this story, which Mathers related on his magical honour as a $7° = 4°$ (the highest grade of the Rosicrucian order), was that Mathers saw double. Crowley, however, was not going to judge any isolated story by the general laws of probability, so, bowing gracefully, he rose and set out to find Allan Bennett, whom he eventually ran down at the house of a holy Yogi in Cinnamon Gardens, Colombo, to hear his account.
>
> Allan Bennett's account was less of a strain upon Aleister Crowley's faculties of belief. They had had, he said, an argument about the God Shiva, the Destroyer, whom Allan Bennett worshipped because, if one repeated his name often enough, Shiva would one day open his eye and destroy the Universe, and whom Mathers feared and hated because He would one day open His eye and destroy Mathers. Allan Bennett closed the argument by assuming the position Padmasana and repeating the Mantra: "Shiva, Shiva, Shiva, Shiva, Shiva, Shiva." Mathers, angrier than ever, sought the sideboard, but soon returned, only to find Allan Bennett still muttering: "Shiva, Shiva, Shiva, Shiva, Shiva". "Will you stop blaspheming?" cried Mathers; but the holy man only said "Shiva, Shiva, Shiva, Shiva, Shiva, Shiva, Shiva, Shiva, Shiva, Shiva." "If you don't stop I will shoot you!" said Mathers, drawing a revolver from his pocket, and levelling it at Allan Bennett's head; but Allan Bennett, being concentrated, took no notice, and continued to mutter "Shiva, Shiva, Shiva, Shiva, Shiva, Shiva."
>
> Whether overawed by the majesty of the saint, or interrupted by the entry of a third person, Allan Bennett no longer remembered, but Mathers never pulled the trigger.
>
> It was only after this interview, which did not take place till August 1901, that Aleister Crowley definitely decided against Mathers.

Is this account accurate?

MATHERS.   "My account is accurate."

SCORPIO, K.C.   You really ask his Lordship to believe this yarn about Abramelin demons?

MATHERS.   Yes.

SCORPIO, K.C.   With regard to Dr. Wynn Westcott, now: was he your colleague?

MATHERS.   Yes.

SCORPIO, K.C. Was his name printed on the MSS. of the Order of the Golden Dawn as the person to whom they should be returned in case of the owner's death or disability?

MATHERS. Yes.

SCORPIO, K.C. And these MSS. contain practical instructions for raising devils, making yourself invisible, transforming men into animals, making gold, making rain, and all the other fabled arts of sorcerers?

MATHERS. Yes.

SCORPIO, K.C. In short, you and Dr. Westcott were teaching the vilest practices of black magic?

MATHERS. Yes.

SCORPIO, K.C. You quarrelled with Dr. Westcott?

MATHERS. Yes.

SCORPIO, K.C. You were jealous of his authority?

MATHERS. Divided authority is no authority?

SCORPIO, K.C. You are not a careless man?

MATHERS. One cannot be too careful in matters of magic.

SCORPIO, K.C. Did you ever leave any magical MSS. in a cab?

MATHERS. The best of us may err. Even Homer nodded.

SCORPIO, K.C. These MSS. were taken to Scotland Yard?

MATHERS. I cannot say, of my own knowledge.

SCORPIO, K.C. That would be the usual course?

MATHERS. I suppose so.

SCORPIO, K.C. Dr. Westcott's name and address being on them, the authorities would return them to him?

MATHERS. I suppose so.

SCORPIO, K.C. Did they further intimate to Dr. Westcott that he was paid to sit on corpses, not to raise them; and that he must choose between his Coronership and his Adeptship?

MATHERS. I believe so.

SCORPIO, K.C. So that he resigned active membership in the so-called Rosicrucian Order?

MATHERS. He did resign.

SCORPIO, K.C. Very fortunate piece of carelessness for you!

MATHERS. Fortune favours the brave.

SCORPIO, K.C. I put it to you, this was a premeditated treachery on your part.

MATHERS. I refuse to answer the question.

SCORPIO, K.C. In your letter of February 16th, 1900, you accuse Dr. Westcott of "forging, or procuring to be forged" the warrant on which the Order was founded?

MATHERS. Yes.

SCORPIO, K.C. And did anyone believe you?

MATHERS. Yes: five persons.

SCORPIO, K.C. Who were they?

MATHERS. Dr. E. W. Berridge, Mr. G. C. Jones, Mr. Aleister Crowley and a Mrs. Simpson and her daughter.

SCORPIO, K.C. What of the other fifty odd in the London Temple?

MATHERS.   Mr. Crowley expelled them.

SCORPIO, K.C.   By what authority?

MATHERS.   By mine. He was at that time my plenipotentiary in London.

SCORPIO, K.C.   And what did they do then?

MATHERS.   They expelled me and Mr. Crowley.

SCORPIO, K.C.   And then?

MATHERS.   They all quarrelled and expelled each other.

SCORPIO, K.C.   The whole Order broke up?

MATHERS.   Yes.

SCORPIO, K.C.   Why did they revolt against you?

MATHERS.   Firstly, because they thought that by declaring the Warrant to be a forgery, I had destroyed my own authority. Secondly, because they couldn't make my methods of magic work properly. Thirdly, because they were tired of my incessant demands for money. Fourthly, because I refused to expel Dr. Berridge from the Order.

SCORPIO, K.C.   What complaints were made against Dr. Berridge?

MATHERS.   That girls who came to him for examination in the Knowledge Lectures were subjected to insult.

SCORPIO, K.C.   Did you investigate this charge?

MATHERS.   "Astrally, yes."

SCORPIO, K.C.   Was there any other charge?

MATHERS.   Yes.

SCORPIO, K.C.   What was it?

MATHERS.   That he was disseminating objectionable literature.

SCORPIO, K.C.   What?

MATHERS.   The works of Thomas Lake Harris.

SCORPIO, K.C.   What is objected to?

MATHERS.   He recommends his pupils to invoke elemental spirits or "astral counterparts" for the purpose of carnal copulation.

SCORPIO, K.C.   Was this charge denied?

MATHERS.   No.

SCORPIO, K.C.   What did you do?

MATHERS.   I expelled his accuser.

SCORPIO, K.C.   Name the accuser.

MATHERS.   Miss Horniman.

SCORPIO, K.C.   The daughter of the great tea merchant?

MATHERS.   The same.

SCORPIO, K.C.   And who is Dr. Berridge?

MATHERS.   He is the famous Dr. Berridge.

SCORPIO, K.C.   For what is he famous?

MATHERS.   For his Magic Clasp.

SCORPIO, K.C.   What is that?

MATHERS.   A Mrs. Cunningham, a member of my Order, claimed £1,000 from him as the price of a Magic Clasp said to have been given by Cagliostro to Marie Antoinette. She sued him on a promissory note for the amount. Her story in court was that she went to his house with a friend on the date when it fell due. Dr. Berridge tried to destroy the note. A struggle ensued: the note was torn, Dr. Berridge retaining the half which bore his alleged signature. In court he declared this signature to be a forgery.

SCORPIO, K.C.   And what did the experts decide?

MATHERS.   They had no means of deciding.

SCORPIO, K.C.   How so?

MATHERS.   Dr. Berridge had burnt his alleged signature.

SCORPIO, K.C.   What? He burnt the proof of his own integrity and of their dishonesty?

MATHERS.   Yes.

SCORPIO, K.C.   How did he account for so extraordinary an action?

MATHERS.   The excitement of the moment.

SCORPIO, K.C.   What did the judge say?

MATHERS.   That it was all very mysterious, that he did not believe either party to the suit; but that as the onus of proof lay on Mrs. Cunningham, he must dismiss the case.

SCORPIO, K.C.   Thank you. Now, has Dr. Berridge any animus against Mr. Crowley?

MATHERS.   Yes.

SCORPIO, K.C.   How has Mr. Crowley wronged him?

MATHERS.   Mr. Crowley has laughed at him.

SCORPIO, K.C.   Anything else?

MATHERS.   Mr. Crowley did him a good turn.

SCORPIO, K.C.   How?

MATHERS.   In March 1910 Mr. Crowley received an anonymous letter from "White Magician" enclosing a pamphlet by T. L. Harris, and accusing Dr. Berridge of the foulest vices.

SCORPIO, K.C.   What did Mr. Crowley do?

MATHERS.   Sent a friend with the letter and pamphlet to Dr. Berridge to warn him that he had an enemy, and offering to help him in any way possible to defeat such anonymous assailants.

SCORPIO, K.C.   Why did Mr. Crowley act thus, if he had no respect for Dr. Berridge?

MATHERS.   He would probably say it was because, however much he disagreed with a man, he would not see him the victim of foul play.

SCORPIO, K.C.   And how did Dr. Berridge repay the service?

MATHERS.   By perjuring himself to Mr. Crowley's disadvantage.

SCORPIO, K.C.   Thank you. Now as to this "Rosicrucian" Order. Let me read to you from the Obligation of a Neophyte:

"All these I swear to keep under the no less penalty than that of. . . . . submitting myself to a deadly and hostile Current of Will set in motion by the Greatly Honoured Chiefs of the Second Order; by which I should fall slain or paralysed, as if blasted by the Lightning Flash." Is that correct?

MATHERS.   Yes.

SCORPIO, K.C.   Is it meant to be taken seriously?

MATHERS.   Yes.

SCORPIO, K.C.   Members of the Order, were, in fact, afraid of the penalty?

MATHERS.   Yes.

SCORPIO, K.C.   On April 2nd, 1900, you write to the revolting members, saying: "I shall for the first time be compelled to formulate my request to the Highest Chiefs to prepare the Punitive Current."

MATHERS.   Yes.

SCORPIO, K.C.   If they refused to obey you, you would cause them "to fall slain or paralysed, as if blasted by the Lightning Flash"?

MATHERS.   They deserved it, and worse.

SCORPIO, K.C.   Is it a threat of assassination?

MATHERS.   Of occult assassination, yes.

SCORPIO, K.C.   You did actually rattle peas in a sieve, ceremonially?

MATHERS.   It is a well-known practice of Sympathetic Magic.

SCORPIO, K.C.   Like sticking pins in a wax figure?

MATHERS.   Exactly. One identifies the rebels with the peas, and rattles them.

SCORPIO, K.C.   That explains their subsequent debâcle?

MATHERS.   Yes.

SCORPIO, K.C.   But you expected them to "fall slain or paralysed"?

MATHERS.   I hoped so.

SCORPIO, K.C.   Actually, not in a figure of speech?

MATHERS.   Actually.

SCORPIO, K.C.   It is attempted assassination?

MATHERS.   Occult assassination, yes.

SCORPIO, K.C.   And in any event, if they were really afraid of it, the threat amounted to black mail?

MATHERS.   I am not a lawyer.

SCORPIO, K.C.   Now then, let us get back to James IV. You say you are James IV?

MATHERS.   "I refuse to answer the question."

SCORPIO, K.C.   James IV was killed on Flodden Field?

MATHERS.   "Tradition asserts that he escaped."

SCORPIO, K.C.   A lady of unblemished reputation, Mrs. Markham, has gone into that box, and sworn that he was so killed.

MATHERS.   One must not contradict a lady.

SCORPIO, K.C.   Well, what happened to him?

MATHERS.   "I – I mean he – escaped to the Continent, and became an Adept and found the Elixir of Life, so that I – I mean he – should live on indefinitely."

SCORPIO, K.C.   When do we hear of him again?

MATHERS.   "As the Comte de St. Germain."

SCORPIO, K.C.   And again?

MATHERS.   "I refuse to answer the question."

SCORPIO, K.C.   Have you read Mr. Crowley's poem: "The Rosicrucian," dedicated "à sa Majesté Jacques IV d'Écosse"?

MATHERS.   Yes. Mr. Crowley was a very young and foolish boy.

SCORPIO, K.C.   He believed you to be James IV?

MATHERS.   Very likely.

SCORPIO, K.C.   Did he or did he not?

MATHERS.   It was not my fault if he didn't.

SCORPIO, K.C.   You borrowed considerable sums of money from him?

MATHERS.   Yes.

SCORPIO, K.C.   On that ground?

MATHERS.   That sort of ground.

SCORPIO, K.C.   He was rich?

MATHERS.   I believe he had just come into some £30,000.

SCORPIO, K.C.   He offered you the whole of his fortune in order to help you in your trouble with the revolting members?

MATHERS.   I wrote to thank him for his "loyal and honourable offer."

SCORPIO, K.C.   Why did he make it?

MATHERS.   He believed my stories about James IV and the Secret Chiefs, I suppose.

SCORPIO, K.C.   Madame Horos had promised you £2,000?

MATHERS.   Yes.

SCORPIO, K.C.   Was that why you admitted her to be your superior?

MATHERS.   I refuse to answer the question.

SCORPIO, K.C.   Crowley offers you his fortune; and you immediately appoint him to the sole power in England, over the heads of Dr. Westcott and Sir Henry Colville and W. B. Yeats and Mrs. Emery and Sir William Crookes and Dr. Berridge and dozens of others who had been members of the Order for years?

MATHERS.   I did.

SCORPIO, K.C.   This is only a coincidence?

MATHERS.   Certainly. I acknowledged Madame Horos because it was a slap in the eye for Mrs. Emery; I gave Crowley the supreme power partly to snub the rebels, and partly (as I said, in another place) "to make a better man of him."

SCORPIO, K.C.   Besides the money that Crowley lent you, did he ever give you any?

MATHERS.   Yes: a wealthy lady, the wife of an English Officer, a Colonel, being interested in occultism, once gave him £20 for me.

SCORPIO, K.C.   Is that all?

MATHERS.   She gave him some jewels for the purpose of decorating a statue of Isis for my temple.

SCORPIO, K.C.   She quarrelled with him subsequently?

MATHERS.   I believe so. In fact, I made quite a big story of it.

SCORPIO, K.C.   They are good friends again, however?

MATHERS.   He has a whole sheaf of the friendliest letters

from her, up to date.

SCORPIO, K.C.   Well, we left Mr. Crowley as your Envoy Plenipotentiary to the "rebels". He shortly afterwards went climbing in Mexico?

MATHERS.   Yes, with Mr. Eckenstein.

SCORPIO, K.C.   What was Mr. Eckenstein's Christian name?

MATHERS.   I – er – I see ladies in Court.

The Judge.   Any ladies in this Court are probably beyond any scruples of that sort.

SCORPIO, K.C.   Answer the question.

MATHERS.   Oscar *(sensation)*.*

SCORPIO, K.C.   Did Mr. Crowley on his departure leave anything in your charge?

MATHERS.   Some books of poetry. I couldn't get a single franc on them: I returned them to him when he came back.

SCORPIO, K.C.   Anything else?

MATHERS.   A fifty-guinea dressing case, and another portmanteau.

SCORPIO, K.C.   Where are they?

MATHERS.   I refuse to answer the question.

SCORPIO, K.C.   Did you return them to the owner?

MATHERS.   No.

SCORPIO, K.C.   In "Konx Om Pax" Mr. Crowley accuses you of stealing these bags?

MATHERS.   He didn't mention the bags specifically. He only said I was a thief. Messrs. Nussey and Fellowes, my Solicitors, wrote threatening him with an Action.

SCORPIO, K.C.   What did he reply?

MATHERS.   "I care as little for your threats of legal action as for your client's threats of assassination. . . . . I am surprised that a firm of your standing should consent to act for a scoundrel".

SCORPIO, K.C.   What did you do?

MATHERS.   I changed my solicitors.

SCORPIO, K.C.   Perhaps it would be more correct to say that your solicitors changed you! You several times threatened Mr. Crowley with legal proceedings?

MATHERS.   Often.

SCORPIO, K.C.   Did you ever take any?

MATHERS.   Once, for breach of copyright.

SCORPIO, K.C.   And tried for an Injunction against the "Equinox"?

MATHERS.   Yes.

SCORPIO, K.C.   What happened?

MATHERS.   Dismissed with costs.

SCORPIO, K.C.   Have you paid those costs?

MATHERS.   No.

SCORPIO, K.C.   Did you then bring the action?

(*) At this point Counsel fainted, and threw up his brief; but was induced to continue by the Judge, who had not had such a jolly day for years.

MATHERS.   No.

SCORPIO, K.C.   It was a frivolous excuse for the injunction?

MATHERS.   I refuse to answer the question. Ask Mr. Cran.

SCORPIO, K.C.   Let me read you this passage from the "Equinox" of September 1910:

> I had almost forgottten dear old Mathers.
>
> Yet it was only last December that a colleague of mine was told by some greasy old harridan, in her best nominal 7° = 4° voice (she has paid hundreds of pounds for that nominal 7° = 4°, and never got initiated into any mysteries but those of Over-eating) that Imperrita (? Imperator, Mathers' title of office in the "Golden Dawn") was coming over from Paris to *crush* Crowley; and Crowley has *fled* before his *face*.
>
> Anyhow, I sneaked back from Algeria, trembling all over, and began to enjoy the comedy of a lawyer pretending that he could not serve a Writ on a man with an address in the telephone directory, who was spending hundreds of pounds on letting the whole world know where to find him. It was perhaps unkind of me not to warn Mr. Cran that he was putting his foot in it.
>
> But if I had said a word, the case would have been thrown up; and then where would our advertisement have been?
>
> So, even now, I restrict my remarks: there may be some more fun coming.
> * * * * *
> But at least there's a prophet loose! Some anonymous person wrote:
>> Cran, Cran, McGregor's man,
>> Served a Writ, and away he ran
>
> before a Writ was served! Though he might have guessed that it would be. But he couldn't possibly have known that the action would be dropped, as it has been. And Mathers has run away too—without paying our costs.
> * * * * *

It reflects seriously upon Mr. Cran's professional honour, does it not?

MATHERS.   Yes.

SCORPIO, K.C.   Has he taken action?

MATHERS.   No.

SCORPIO, K.C.   So Mr. Crowley laughed at you?

MATHERS.   Those who laugh last laugh best.

SCORPIO, K.C.   What did you do?

MATHERS.   I waited for my opportunity.

SCORPIO, K.C.   Did it arrive?

MATHERS.   All things come to him who waits.

SCORPIO, K.C.   Describe what happened.

MATHERS.   A paper called "The Looking Glass" attacked Mr. Crowley. I went to the editor (Mr. W. F. de Wend Fenton) and told him all I knew – and a good deal that I didn't know.

SCORPIO, K.C.   Was the editor actuated by malice against Mr. Crowley?

MATHERS.   No.

SCORPIO, K.C.   How can you be sure?

MATHERS.   The day after his first article appeared he telephoned to a mutual friend, a Miss O. . ., explained that he meant no harm, and would like to meet Mr. Crowley at dinner and have a chat with him.

SCORPIO, K.C.   What happened then?

MATHERS.   Miss O. . . told Mr. Crowley.

SCORPIO, K.C.   And what did he say?

MATHERS.   He made an answer so remarkable that I remember it every word.

SCORPIO, K.C.   What was it?

MATHERS.  He said "I suppose you wouldn't like me to be blackmailed over your coffee".

SCORPIO, K.C.  What does this show?

MATHERS.  Mr. Crowley's horrid suspicious temper.

SCORPIO, K.C.  What did Miss O. . . do?

MATHERS.  Cut Mr. Fenton.

SCORPIO, K.C.  You really know all this of your own knowledge?

MATHERS.  Yes.

SCORPIO, K.C.  How?

MATHERS.  "Astrally."

SCORPIO, K.C.  Astrally?

MATHERS.  "I am the Head of the Rosicrucian Order."

SCORPIO, K.C.  Did Mr. Crowley take action against "The Looking-Glass"?

MATHERS.  No.

SCORPIO, K.C.  Why?

MATHERS.  On the advice of a friend with 25 years' experience of City Journalism.

SCORPIO, K.C.  What did the friend say?

(Counsel objected. A long argument followed, in the course of which the Judge remarked: "This trial is like the trial in Alice in Wonderland. I wouldn't spoil it for the world and I am going to admit anything!").

SCORPIO, K.C.  What did Mr. Crowley's journalistic friend say?

MATHERS.  "Let the fellow alone! He's been warned off the turf, and his City Editor's a jail-bird, and he isn't worth a bob, and if you touch pitch you'll be defiled."

SCORPIO, K.C.  Was Mr. Fenton in fact warned off the Turf?

MATHERS.  Yes.

SCORPIO, K.C.  You blame Crowley for not taking action?

MATHERS. It's very annoying.

SCORPIO, K.C. You're not very ready to take action yourself?

MATHERS.  I am a man of peace.

SCORPIO, K.C.  The "military bearing" is only for show?

MATHERS.  That's all.

SCORPIO, K.C.  Mr. Crowley has written books, which houses of the highest standing have published, in which you are openly called a common thief, an habitual swindler, a blackmailer, and accused of drunkenness and attempted assassination?

MATHERS.  Yes: but he supports his charges by unimpeachable documents, and witnesses of unassailable integrity.

SCORPIO, K.C.  And there is no ground for the charges against Mr. Crowley?

MATHERS.  There is Dr. Berridge's evidence.

SCORPIO, K.C.  Let us go into that. Mr. Crowley's conversation with Dr. Berridge took place in 1900?

MATHERS.  Yes.

SCORPIO, K.C.  And was first repeated in the Court of King's Bench in 1911?

MATHERS. Yes.

SCORPIO, K.C. Dr. Berridge must have a splendid memory. What were the relations between Crowley and Berridge in 1904?

MATHERS. They were friends and colleagues. At the Ceremony of the Vernal Equinox in 1903 Crowley was Hierophant, and Berridge Praemonstrator or Cancellarius, I forget which.

SCORPIO, K.C. So it took Dr. Berridge some time before he attached a criminal significance to Crowley's remark?

MATHERS. The mind of Berridge works slowly, but it works exceeding small.

SCORPIO, K.C. As to the remark itself. Take the first part. Berridge mentions to Crowley the ugly rumours that his enemies were circulating. Crowley replies: "So and So and So and So and So and So have been to my flat and passed the night." I suggest that the names mentioned were those of mutual friends of Crowley and Berridge, men beyond suspicion.

MATHERS. It may have been so.

SCORPIO, K.C. And that Crowley added, implicitly or explicitly: "Is that any reason for making such abominable charges?"

MATHERS. Perhaps.

SCORPIO, K.C. I must ask you to remember that Crowley was brought up among the Plymouth Brethren, and that at this time he had no more knowledge of the world than most boys of 16. He swallowed your yarns easily enough, didn't he?

MATHERS. He did.

SCORPIO, K.C. Now take the second part. "For the last eighteen months or two years there has been nothing that the police could get at me for." That implies that previous to that date there was something?

MATHERS. Undoubtedly.

SCORPIO, K.C. Let me read you this passage from Crowley's works Vol. I, p. 115, published in 1903: Sonnets. . . . . . . To the author of the phrase "I am not a gentleman, and I have no friends."

> "Self-damned, the leprous moisture of thy veins
> Sickens the sunshine, and thine haggard eyes,
> Bleared with their own corrupting infamies,
> Glare through the charnel-house of earthly
> pains,
> Horrible as already in hell. . . . . .
> Self-damned on earth, live out thy tortured days
> That men may look upon thy face, and see
> How vile a thing of woman born may be. . . . . ."

I need not continue. But I will read the foot-note of Mr. Ivor Back, F.R.C.S., the Editor:

> "The virulence of these sonnets is excusable when it is known that their aim was to destroy the influence in Cambridge of a man who headed in that University a movement parallel to that which at Oxford was associated with the name of Oscar Wilde."

It is clear from this that Crowley had been associated with a man of bad character; but that on discovering him to be so, he instantly disowned him?

MATHERS. Yes.

SCORPIO, K.C. Mr. Crowley may have thought that even an innocent association with such a person was criminal?

MATHERS. He was very young and foolish.

SCORPIO, K.C. It is this that he referred to in his remark to Dr. Berridge?

MATHERS. May be.

SCORPIO, K.C. The date tallies?*

MATHERS. Yes.

SCORPIO, K.C. And that is all there is against Mr. Crowley?

MATHERS. There is "The Sword of Song."

SCORPIO, K.C. What is that?

MATHERS. Out of some hundreds of marginal notes, there are two (some say four) the initials of whose words make other most improper words.**

SCORPIO, K.C. Did anyone discover this before you did?

MATHERS. Not to my knowledge.

SCORPIO, K.C. Did Captain Fuller in his three years' laborious study of Mr. Crowley's works discover it?

MATHERS. No.

SCORPIO, K.C. Is there any point in these – do you call them jokes?

MATHERS. No point at all.

SCORPIO, K.C. Are Mr. Crowley's jokes usually pointless?

MATHERS. Alas, no!

SCORPIO, K.C. And did not the reviewers discover this?

MATHERS. Unfortunately, no. On the contrary, Mr. G. K. Chesterton wrote a column in the *Daily News*, in which the book is treated as a serious contribution to Philosophy.

SCORPIO, K.C. Is there anything else?

MATHERS. There's the "Mother's Tragedy."

SCORPIO, K.C. What is that?

MATHERS. A book of poems one of which deals with a subject which I blush to mention.

SCORPIO, K.C. Has any wretch previously dealt with it?

MATHERS. Yes.

SCORPIO, K.C. Who?

MATHERS. Sophocles in Oedipus Rex; Shakespeare in Hamlet and in Pericles; Malory in Morte d'Arthur; Byron in Parisina, Manfred, and other poems; Shelley in the Cenci, Rosalind and Helen, and in Laon and Cythna; Wilde in Salome; Ford in The Unnatural Combat and 'Tis Pity she's a Whore; Moses, Wagner, Schiller, Alfieri, and many other authors of the highest reputation.

SCORPIO, K.C. But Mr. Crowley tries to sell his works by printing reviews which describe them as "revolting"?

MATHERS. Yes, that's the bad part.

SCORPIO, K.C. Has not Mr. Crowley habitually reprinted all

(*) The poem (not the foot-note) was first published in 1899, having been written during one of the eclipses in late '98 or early '99.

(**) For an example of what this kind of criticism may lead to, *vide* Appendix.

sorts of reviews of his works, good and bad, with a giant's contempt for reviewers?

MATHERS.   Of course.

SCORPIO, K.C.   But was this particular review really so unfavourable?

MATHERS.   Not at all; but by picking out a single sentence, I made it appear so.

SCORPIO, K.C.   What about these aliases of his? Why did he assume the name of MacGregor?

MATHERS.   At my suggestion. He was about to take a house in Scotland, and I thougt it would attract less remark if he took a Highland name.

SCORPIO, K.C.   But why MacGregor rather than any other Highland name?

MATHERS.   To assert an "astral link" – what you might call a bond of sympathy – between himself and me. He had gone there to perform a magical operation detailed in a book which I had just published.

SCORPIO, K.C.   He was at this time quite under your auspices?

MATHERS.   Under my thumb.

SCORPIO, K.C.   And why did he call himself Lord Boleskine?

MATHERS.   Principally to annoy the snobbish society of Inverness.

SCORPIO, K.C.   And did it annoy them?

MATHERS.   I believe so.

SCORPIO, K.C.   But why Lord Boleskine?

MATHERS.   He is the Laird of Boleskine, and Laird is only Scots for Lord.

SCORPIO, K.C.   And why did he call himself Count Svareff?

MATHERS.   In the book of mine I referred to it says that the Aspirant to the Sacred Magic would be much annoyed by his family seeking to dissuade him. So he changed his name and disappeared.

SCORPIO, K.C.   Why Svareff?

MATHERS.   The romantic young idiot had just come back from Russia.

SCORPIO, K.C.   Why Count?

MATHERS.   All Russians are Counts, I believe, when they're not Princes!

SCORPIO, K.C.   You say he obtained a large sum of money from a celebrated singer?

MATHERS.   Yes.

SCORPIO, K.C.   A married woman?

MATHERS.   Yes.

SCORPIO, K.C.   Of what age? You must remember that Crowley was a mere boy.

MATHERS.   Ten or fifteen years older than Crowley.

SCORPIO, K.C.   On what pretext did he obtain the money?

MATHERS.   She proposed to Crowley to go with her to Texas, divorce her husband, and marry him.

SCORPIO, K.C.   What did Crowley do?

MATHERS.   He gave her a fifty-guinea engagement ring.

SCORPIO, K.C.   Did the scheme come off?

MATHERS.   No.

SCORPIO, K.C.   Did she return the ring?

MATHERS.   Crowley complains in the Sword of Song that she did not.

SCORPIO, K.C.   And what about his obtaining money from her?

MATHERS.   Oh! that's only my fun.

SCORPIO, K.C.   You mean it's a lie?

MATHERS.   Well, it's not true.

SCORPIO, K.C.   Is that all you have against Crowley?

MATHERS.   No: he was divorced from his wife.

SCORPIO, K.C.   What was his fault?

MATHERS.   Chivalry.

SCORPIO, K.C.   Give the facts.

MATHERS.   They are known to all Mr. Crowley's intimate friends, who approve his action throughout, and they may be surmised from the poem ''Rosa Decidua'' published in ''The Winged Beetle''. But the facts being detailed in Mr. Crowley's petition for the reduction of the decree of divorce, they cannot be entered into more fully at this moment; and as the unhappy lady became insane in September, 1911, I think we may well leave the matter in its tragic silence.

SCORPIO, K.C.   Then Mr. Crowley was not to blame?

MATHERS.   Not in this matter. But he is an associate of the notorious Jones.

SCORPIO, K.C.   Oh, well! we won't go into that. Thank you.

## APPENDIX

## MY CRAPULOUS PREDECESSORS

### No. I.

### ROBERT BROWNING

[The method of critical analysis is not our own, who reverence Robert Browning as one of the greatest of the Victorian Poets. It is borrowed, with the acknowledgment of inverted commas (even the commas!) from distinguished luminaries of the Bench and Bar. ED.]

("I have some hesitation" in printing "the following, as I see ladies" waiting at the booksellers'. S. C. H.

"Any ladies" waiting at the booksellers' "are probably far beyond any scruples of that sort." Mr. Justice Mutton.)

### PIPPA PASSES, BY ROBERT BROWNING.

"I would call your lordship's attention very particularly to the initial letters of" of this obscene and revolting poem." Separately: how every Englishman must shudder and vomit at "the loathsome and abominable creature who has the effrontery to" have been dead and buried without giving posterity "a chance to cross-examine him"! Together: how every Frenchman must cry "Faugh! Ugh! Ugh! Faugh!" and blush! Transpose two vowels only: what hideous and filthy anagram springs to sight! "If this is accidental, Mr." Browning "is a very unfortunate man; if it is intentional, no words of mine can be strong enough to denounce the loathsome and abominable character of this book." But can it be accidental? Was not Mr. Browning a friend – a friend! – of that Mr. Scrutton whose name is an anagram of a sentence – not merely a word, mark you! – which asserts a pathological fact familiar to every Syphilographer and his clients, couched in the crudest and coarsest language!

And if this be an accident too, what shall we say of the infamous examples of paraprodokian from the plain text itself?

"Æsculapius, an Epic. Catalogue of the drugs: Hebe's plaister – One strip cools your lip. Phœbus' emulsion – One bottle clears your throttle. Mercury's bolus – one box cures . . ."

And –

> "I have made her gorge polenta
> Till her cheeks are both as bouncing
> As her – name there's no pronouncing!"

And what of the whole scheme of the poem?

The chief character is a vile procurer who is trying to sell Pippa into the White Slave Traffic.

The first episode deals most realistically with adultery crowned by murder.

The second episode describes a plot to marry an innocent youth to a harlot.

The third episode shows a mother trying to prevent her son from committing a murder in cold blood, and failing to do so. This assassination has the open approval of the "so-called poet."

And "the loathsome and abominable creature" who "disseminates this unutterable filth" was allowed to die in peace! "Where were the police? What were they about to let him escape" to Italy?

Italy, indeed! This horrible creature dedicates "his best intentions" (I'm sorry I can't think of any bad meaning for H.B.I.) "affectionately to Mr. Sergeant Talfourd." Affectionately, mark the word! What do such "loathsome and abominable creatures" mean by affection? Gentlemen of the jury, if this Mr. *(sic)* Sergeant (save the mark!) Talfourd (Ugh!) had come to court to ask you to clear him from a blackmailer's libel, you would have known how to brand him with everlasting infamy!

S. C. HILLER.

Villa – and
Family –
in part!

# Abbey Unnatural

*Opposite*: Alostrael (Leah), Crowley and the doomed baby Poupée at the Abbey in 1921. The two little boys are Dionysus, Leah's son, and Hermes, the child of Crowley and Ninette Fraux, his Second Concubine.

*Below*: The Scarlet Woman's visiting card.

The Great Beast's Abbey of Thelema in Cefalù, Sicily never quite lived up to the dream-image of it in his novel *The Diary Of A Drug Fiend* (1922). It was an unsanitary hovel, fraught by arguments, deaths (of Crowley's child Poupée and of Raoul Loveday) and, finally, Crowley's expulsion by Mussolini. But there is no doubt he was happy there and that it has an important place in the Crowley legend.

In 1955 filmmaker Kenneth Anger went to Cefalù to make a sound documentary on the Abbey and to uncover the many demonic Crowley paintings on the walls of the ruin, hidden beneath layers of whitewash. The pictures which follow include many taken at that time.

*The Scarlet Woman*

*Alostrael 31 666·31*

*Abbey of Thelema*

*Left*: Disciple Jane Wolfe (left) and Leah at the Abbey.

*Above and below*: The Abbey in its setting. Crowley banished recalcitrant disciples to the big rock in the background.

*Above*: Demon on the wall of the Chamber of Horrors, Crowley's bedroom.

*Below*: Kenneth Anger shows US sexologist Professor Kinsey around.

*Above*: Another painting from the bedroom, allegedly of Leah.

The Abbey was
exorcised after
Crowley departed
and the walls were
whitewashed, hiding
all the paintings like
the pornographic
mural (*opposite*).
Kenneth Anger had
to painstakingly
remove all of this,
and a thick layer of
cement to expose the
Magic Circle on the
floor of the Sanctum
Sanctorum,
Crowley's temple
(*right*).

*Right*: Kenneth
Anger examining
work in progress on
paint removal from a
set of shutters. In the
background, a door is
inscribed with the
Crowley creed, 'Do
What Thou Wilt'.

*Opposite*: Female disciples were branded (or painted) with the Mark of the Beast. This is Leila Waddell, also with violin (*above*).

*Top right*: Raoul Loveday, the disciple who died.

*Right*: The young Beast with magickal implements in pre-Abbey days.

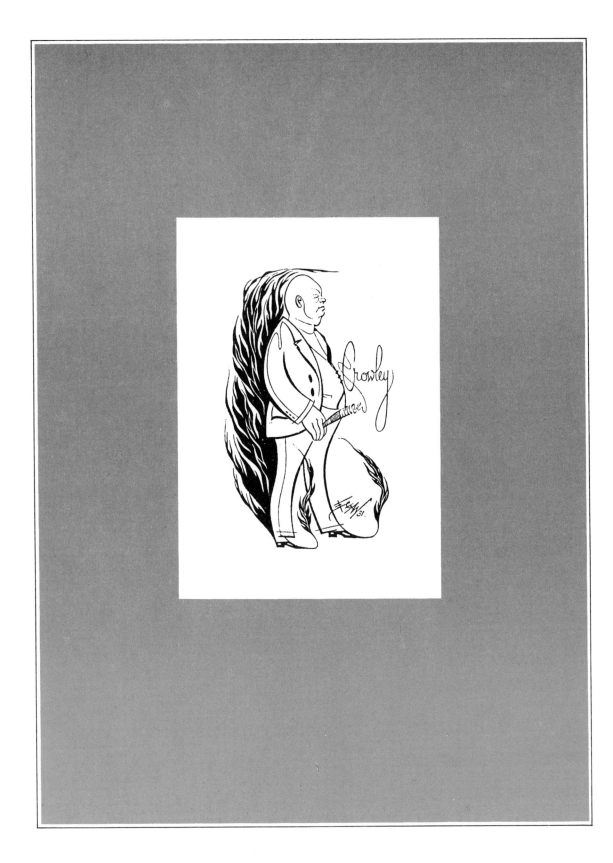

# The Fictional Crowley

It's hardly surprising that a character as strangely charismatic as Aleister Crowley has inspired a number of authors to base novels and short-stories on his exploits. Occasionally Crowley appears under his own name, as in the semi-pornographic fiction *Memoir Of Aleister Crowley* (1967) by James Harvey, or merely in spirit, as is the case with Eric Ericson's novel *Master Of The Temple* (1983), a magickal morality tale which manages to mix a good deal of occult lore with an excess of detail on the business of biscuit manufacturing!

Occult fiction, of course, is plentiful – ranging from the classics of Bulwer-Lytton to the Golden Dawn-inspired pornographic ramblings of Joel Harris's *Inpenetrable* (sic-n.d.) – but that dealing with Crowley-based characters is virtually a sub-genre by itself. The list overleaf is not exhaustive, but includes only those examples of Crowley-based characters whose provenance is pretty much beyond dispute. There's no doubt that Maugham's Haddo, for instance, is the Crowley he knew in Paris early this century. Crowley could easily have sued, but decided instead to adopt 'Haddo' as one of his pseudonyms! The physical and circumstantial descriptions of the James and Wakefield protagonists make it quite clear that it is Crowley we are dealing with, while Dion Fortune's Astley is obviously her ex-colleague of the Golden Dawn painted black.

Both Wellman and Colin Wilson have stated that their respective villains are Crowley-based, though in Wilson's book Cunningham is said to be a disciple of the Beast. The portrait is unmistakable, however, as it is with all the thinly-disguised Crowleys listed here. According to Crowley himself, Elphenor Pistouillat de la Ratisboisière, the hero of a book of short tales titled *The Deuce and All* by George Raffalovich, is a Crowley-based character. There are also Crowleyan echoes in much modern speculative fiction: R A Wilson has used him as an anti-hero, while Heinlein's *Stranger In A Strange Land* is tinged with his philosophy.

The following table shows the use made of an Aleister Crowley-based character by various authors.

*Above*: Crowley attends a literary luncheon, seated next to an effigy of the murderer Charlie Peace.

| Author | Story | Crowley-character |
| --- | --- | --- |
| Somerset Maugham | *The Magician* | Oliver Haddo |
| M R James | *Casting The Runes* | Karswell |
| H R Wakefield | *He Cometh And He Passeth By* | Oscar Clinton |
| " " " | *A Black Solitude* | Apuleius Charlton |
| Dion Fortune | *The Winged Bull* | Hugo Astley |
| Manly Wade Wellman | *Thorne On The Threshold*, et al | Rowley Thorne |
| Colin Wilson | *Man Without A Shadow* | Caradoc Cunningham |
| Anthony Powell | *Dance To The Music Of Time* novels | Dr Trelawney Scorpio Murtlock |
| Dennis Wheatley | *The Devil Rides Out* | Mocata |
| James Blish | *Black Easter* | Theron Ware |

*Above*: James Blish's distinctly Crowleyan novel, *Black Easter*.

*Left*: Modern edition of Somerset Maugham's *The Magician*, based on Crowley. Some said Maugham had signed a pact with Crowley to obtain fame.

LOVECRAFT & RAVEN

The OCCULT LOVECRAFT

# The Lovecraft/Crowley Axis

*Opposite*: Cover of one of the many books linking the late writer HP Lovecraft with occult traditions.

The late H P Lovecraft (1890–1937) was one of the finest exponents of occult horror fiction, and yet he was a confirmed rationalist who had no patience with any kind of mystical hoo-hah in his everyday life. For him, magickal lore was just something to be used in heightening the suspense in his tales and nothing more. However, even his friend Frank Belknap Long – who more or less accepts Lovecraft's materialist stance – has said: 'He was a dreamer on the nightside, an explorer of the Great Unknown in a Blakean sense, *whether he knew it or not.*' (my italics)

Several scholars have seized on this idea – that Lovecraft may have been in touch with occult entities without being consciously aware of it – to get round the man's denial of magick. The most interesting of these theorists is Crowley's disciple Kenneth Grant, who (in books such as *Outside The Circles Of Time* and *Cults Of The Shadow*) has noted uncanny similarities between various aspects of Crowleyanity and Lovecraft's fictions, putting forward the notion that Lovecraft was truly in touch with other spheres of being. In his book *The Magical Revival* he even drew up a table of comparisons: H P Lovecraft's mythical 'grimoire', *The Necronomicon* (or *Al Azif*) versus Aleister Crowley's *Book Of The Law* (or *Al vel Legis*); Lovecraft's 'Great Old Ones' versus the Golden Dawn's 'Great Ones Of The Night Of Time', referred to in the Golden Dawn's rituals, and so on.

The publication, in 1976, of the fifth volume of H P Lovecraft's *Selected Letters* by Arkham House spurred the controversy: on page 120 Lovecraft mentions Crowley, albeit in derogatory fashion, and one of the H R Wakefield tales based on him. This was the first time scholars had seen any evidence that Lovecraft had heard of the Beast, although in his *Supernatural Horror In Literature* essay he had reviewed *The Dark Chamber*, a novel by Leonard Cline which mentions Crowley in its pages.

# Iff . . .

*Opposite*: The late
Beresford Egan's
beautiful artwork for
the jacket of
Crowley's Simon Iff
novel, *Moonchild*.

Crowley was not above utilising himself as a fictional
character: in *The Diary Of A Drug Fiend* he is the misunder-
stood genius-mystic King Lamus, while in *Moonchild* he
appears as the strange and idealised Simon Iff. Crowley
penned a series of short tales starring Iff, several of which
appeared in the American-based German-propaganda magazine *The International* during the First World War. These
tales are among the rarest of Crowley's writings, and this is
certainly the first time the following has appeared in book
form.

## Big Game

Dick Ffoulkes was in good practice at the Criminal Bar,
and his envied dinner parties, given to few and well-
known friends, were nearly always held in his chambers in
Lincoln's Inn. They looked out on one of the pleasantest
green spots in London.

There was a brooding of fog on the first December night of
1911, when Ffoulkes gave a supper to celebrate his victory
over the Crown in the matter of the Marsden murder.

Marsden was a wealthy man, and had no enemies. The
police suspected a mere protege of his unmarried sister,
who was his only heir; he might thus benefit indirectly; no
other motive could be found. The boy – for he was barely
twenty – had dined with Marsden on the night of the
murder, and of course the police had finger-prints by the
dozen. Ffoulkes had torn their flimsy web to rags, and
tossed them in the air with a laugh.

All his guests had gone but one, his oldest friend, Jack
Flynn. They dated from Rugby, and had continued their
inseparability at Balliol. They had read together for the bar,
but Flynn, after being called, had branched off into the
higher journalism.

The Marsden case had stirred England profoundly.
Slight as was the motive attributed to Ezra Robinson, the
suspected boy, there was no other person with any motive at all; faint as were the clues which pointed to him,
there were none at all to point elsewhere.

Besides these considerations, there was apparently no
physical possibility of any other murderer. Marsden had
unquestionably died of a thrust in the heart from a common carving-knife, which was identified as the one which

had been sent up with the dinner. Unobserved access to
the suite was impossible, a floor clerk being continuously
seated in full view of the only door to the whole apart-
ment. The only person known to have been in the room,
after the table had been cleared by the hotel servants,
was the accused. And even Ffoulkes had not dared to
suggest that the wound – a straight drive from above and
behind – might have been self-inflicted. Nor was there any
motive of robbery, or any trace of search for papers. But
there was an undoubted thumb-print of Robinson's in
blood on the handle of the carving knife, and there was a
cut on his left hand. He had explained this, and the
presence of the knife itself, by saying that he had slipped
as he was carving, and that he had run into the bathroom
to wash and bind the cut, leaving the knife on the wash-
tand.

The only point clean for the defense was the medical
evidence, which put the time of death some two hours
later than the departure of Robinson. This coincided with a
temporary failure of the electric current all through the
hotel. Ffoulkes suggested that the old man, who had
drunk a good deal of wine, had gone to take a bath before
retiring, seen the knife, remembered his old skill as an
amateur juggler, ample testimony of which was forthcoming, and started to play at catching the knife. The light
had gone out while he was throwing; he had dodged
maladroitly, and the blade had chanced to catch him
between the shoulders.

The opposite theory was that Robinson had returned to
fetch his cigarette-case, which was in fact found in the

97

room by the police, passed the floor clerk and slipped into the suite in the short spell of darkness, seen his opportunity and seized it, making off before the light was restored. He had not been able to give a satisfactory account of his movements. His story was that he had left Marsden early on account of a severe headache, and had wandered about the streets trying to obtain relief; on the other hand, no one in the hotel would swear to having seen him after his ostensible departure. The floor clerk had testified to a considerable commotion just at the time of the failure of the electric supply: she had heard noises apparently in several rooms; but this might well have been the normal confusion caused by the sudden darkness.

Flynn had been of the utmost service to Ffoulkes in the case. He had performed a weekly miracle in avoiding a spell of prison for contempt of court; for every week he had returned to the charge. There were long articles on miscarriages of justice; others on the weakness of circumstantial evidence where no strong motive was evident; others again on strange accidental deaths. He quoted the case of Professor Milnes Marshall, who slipped and fell while setting up his camera in Deep Ghyll on Scawfell. He was on a gentle slope of snow, yet he made no effort to recover himself, and rolled over and over to the edge of a precipice, at whose foot he was found dead, smashed to a pulp. This happened in full view of several other climbers. This accident was contrasted with that of Arthur Wellman on the Trifthorn. He fell eight hundred feet, and yet only hurt himself by cutting his leg slightly with his ice axe.

A hundred such parallels were at the service of Flynn, and he hammered them into the head of the public week by week, while scrupulously avoiding any reference to Marsden. As the courts had no idea, officially, of the line of the defense, they could say nothing. But Flynn moulded the opinion of the public soundly and shrewdly, and in the end the jury had acquitted Robinson after a bare quarter of an hour's deliberation.

Ffoulkes' guests had complimented him on the ingenuity of his theory of an accident, but the lawyer had not been pleased. "That was a frill," he had replied; "the real defense was Absence of Motive. Grant the police their theory of Robinson's movements: put the knife in his hand, and a certain get-away – which he had not got, mind you; the light might have come on any second – but allow everything, and then ask yourselves: "Why should he stab the man?" There was no quarrel; his marriage with Miss Marsden was not opposed; on the contrary he risked that marriage by a mix-up of this sort; yet we are to suppose that he did it on the mere chance that there would be no fuss, and that his fiancée would have twelve thousand a year instead of four. Why a sane man would hardly kill a rabbit on such motive!"

But now the guests were gone; Ffoulkes and Flynn lit fresh cigars, and settled down for an honest talk. At the elbow of each stood a bottle of the Green Seal '63, one of the soundest wines that ever came out of Oporto. For some time they smoked in silence.

"This is capital wine, Dick," said Flynn presently.

"Ah, cher ami, it is only ten years older than we are. We are getting to the port and portly stage of life."

"Well, there are thrills left. This has been a great case."

"Yes. I'm glad you stayed. I thought you might care to hear about it."

"Hear about it!"

"Yes, there were interesting features."

"But we need hardly recapitulate."

"Oh, I don't mean what came out at the trial."

"No? . . . I suppose nothing ever does come out at a trial!"

"Just as nothing ever gets into the newspapers."

"All right. Spit it out. I suppose Robinson did it, for a start."

"Of course. There was an accident in it, but one of a different kind. When the elevator put him out on Marsden's floor, he was amazed to recognize an old flame in that very prepossessing floor clerk Maud Duval. They had been members of some kind of devil-worhip club, and one of their games was cocaine. Robinson's a perfect fiend, by the way; we had to smuggle the stuff in to him all the time he was in prison, or he'd have gone crazy. Well, the old passion lit like tinder. They had lost each other somehow – you know how such things happen – both had made desperate efforts to renew the link, but in vain. So he told her his plans in ten words. Her answer was equally sweet and to the point. 'Kill the old man – I'll cover your tracks; marry the old girl; and meet me at our old trysting-place at midnight a year from to-day. We'll find a way to be rid of her. Don't risk another word till then.' Great and successful criminals have always this faculty of firmness of character and promptitude of decision. The rest of the story is short. The knife incident was intentional; for Robinson had brought no weapon. He left the hotel openly at nine-thirty; came in again by the bar entrance, went unnoticed to the mezzanine floor, and thence to Marsden's floor, thus avoiding the notice of the main office. The failure of the electricity had nothing to do with it – happened twenty minutes later. He walked in, killed the old man, and left as he had come. Pretty bold? Only cocaine. So now he's off to marry old Miss Marsden's money."

"I begin to see some sort of motive! Maud is what they call 'some peach' across the Straits of America."

"Yes; a perfect devil, with the face of a baby, and the manners of the jeune fille bien élevée. Just such a woman as you are a man, Jack, you old scoundrel."

"Many thanks. I think your own morals – in this case – have been a trifle open to criticism. I suppose it's your fifteen years of law."

"No; it's being under the influence of dear old Jack, with his fifteen years of journalism!"

"Stop rotting! I'm a bit staggered, you know, straight. Let's have another bottle of port."

Ffoulkes went to the buttery, and returned with a couple. For ten minutes neither spoke.

"I've a damned funny feeling," said Flynn at last. "Do you remember the night we put the iodide of nitrogen in the Doctor's nighties?"

"By the soft leather of this chair, I do!"

"Yes; we caught it! But it's the spirit, not the flesh, which goads me now. I've loved skating around the judges, these last weeks. The best thing in life is the feeling of escape. It's the one real thrill. Perhaps that's why I've always been so keen on solitary climbing and big game shooting.''

''I always preferred fishing. My thrill comes from proving my intellectual stamina or subtlety.'' There was a pause.

''What do you think of murder, anyhow?'' suddenly blurted out the journalist.

''The most serious crime, except high treason, known to the English law.''

''True, O wise judge! But what is it morally?''

''An art, according to that ass Wilde.''

''When I write an essay on it, I shall treat it as a sport. And between you and me, that is why I have never written one.''

''Why?''

''Why, old intellectual stamina and subtlety, because if I ever do take it up, I don't want some fool to fix me up with a motive. But after your story of to-night, I don't mind telling you; if I'm caught, I'll brief you! Observe, O man of motives, the analysis. Man is no longer killed for food, except in distant countries, or in rare emergencies such as shipwreck.''

''He is only killed nowadays for one of two motives, gain or revenge.''

''Add love.''

''That's psychopathic.''

''Well, we're all psychopaths; it's only a term of endearment in common use among doctors.''

''Get on!''

''But there's the greatest motive of all – adventure. We've standardized life too much; and those of us who love life are more and more driven to seek adventure in crime.''

''Or journalism.''

''Which is only one of the meaner crimes. But you needn't talk; the practice of law is the nearest thing we have to man-hunting.''

''I suppose that's true.''

''Of course it's true. But it's a mere pheasant-shoot, with all your police for beaters. The game hasn't a chance. No. The motiveless murderer has the true spirit of sport; to kill a man is more dangerous than to follow a wounded gaur into the jungle. The anarchist goes after the biggest game of all: but he's not a sportsman; he has a genuine grievance.''

''Your essay on murder will make some very pleasant reading.''

''But doesn't it attract you too, with your passion to prove your mental superiority to others? Think of the joy of baffling the stupid police, fooling the detectives with false clues, triumphantly proving yourself innocent when you know you are guilty!''

''Are you tempting me? You always did, you know.''

''Anyhow, you always fell!''

''Cher ami, for that alone I could forgive you everything!''

''Sarcastic to the last!''

''You have me to thank that we usually escaped the consequences!''

''Pride, my poor friend!''

''Truth, comrade in misfortune!''

''No. Seriously. I'm crazy to-night, and I really am going to tempt you. Don't prove it's my fault, blame your own good port, and also certain qualities in your own story of the Marsden case. One or two little remarks of yours on the subject of Miss Maud Duval –''

''I knew something would come of that.''

''Yes, that's my weak point. I'm absurdly feminine in vanity and love of power over – a friend.''

''Now I'm warned; so fire ahead. What's the proposal?''

''Oh, I haven't thought of that yet!''

''You big baby!''

''Yes, it's my bedtime; I'll roll home, I think.''

''No, don't go. Let's sober up on coffee, and the '48 brandy.''

''It's a damned extraordinary thing that a little brandy makes you drunk, and a lot of it straightens you out again.''

''It's Providence!''

''Then call upon it in the time of trouble!''

Ffoulkes went in search of the apparatus. Jack rose lazily and went to the window; he threw it open, and the cold damp air came in with a rush. It was infinitely pleasurable, the touch on his heated, wine-flushed face.

He stood there for perhaps ten minutes. A voice recalled him to himself.

''Cafē noir, Gamiani!''

He started as if he had been shot. Ffoulkes, in an embroidered dressing gown of black silk, was seated on cushions on the floor, gravely pouring Turkish coffee from a shining pot of hammered brass.

At one side of him was a great silver hookah, its bowl already covered by a coal from the fire.

Jack took a second dressing-gown that had been thrown across his chair, and rapidly made himself at ease. Then he seated himself opposite to his friend; bowed deeply, with joined hands upon his forehead, and said with mock solemnity: ''Be pleased to say thy pleasure, O most puissant king!''

''Let Scherezade recount the mirific tale of the Two Thousand and Second Night, wherein it is narrated how the wicked journalist tempted the good lawyer in the matter of murder regarded as a pastime and as a debating society!''

''Hearing and obedience! But I must have oh! such a lot of this coffee before I get wound up!''

As it happened, it was two hours before Jack deigned to speak. ''To use the phrase of Abdullah El Haji i-Shiraz,'' he began, ''I remove the silken tube of the rose-perfumed huqqa from my mouth. When King Brahmadatta reigned in Benares, there were two brothers named Chuckerrbutty Lal and Hari Ramkrishna. For short we shall call them Pork and Beans. Now Pork, who was a poet and a devil of a fine fellow, was tempted by the reprobate Beans, a lawyer, whose only quality was low cunning, to join him in a wager. And these were the terms thereof. During the season of the monsoon each was to go away from Benares to a far country, and there he was feloniously and of his malice aforethought, to kill and murder a liege of the Sultan of that land. And when they returned, they were to compare their stories. It was agreed that such murder should be a real murder in the legal sense – an act for which they would be assuredly hanged if they were caught; and also that it would be contrary to the spirit of sport to lay false trails deliberately, and so put in peril the life of some innocent person, not being the game desired to fill the bag. But it must be an undoubted murder, with no possibility of suicide or accident. The murder, moreover, must be of a purely adventurous nature, not a crime inspired by greed or animosity. The idea was to prove that it would be perfectly safe, since there would be no motive to draw suspicion upon them. Yet if either were suspected of the mamelukes, the Sbirri, the janissaries, or the proggins, he should take refuge with the other; but – mark this, O king! – for being so clumsy he should pay to him a camel-load of gold, which in our money is one thousand pounds. Is it a bet?''

Ffoulkes extended his hand. ''It's a bet.''

''You're really game?''

''Dying oath.''

''Dying oath. And now, O king, for I perceive that thou art weary, hie thee to thy chaste couch, and thy faithful slave shall doss it on the sofa.''

In the morning Ffoulkes said, over the breakfast-table, ''About that bet.'' ''It's on?'' cried Flynn in alarm. ''Oh, yes! Only–er – I suppose I need about another seven or eight years of law; I stipulate that – what is thrown away – shall be as worthless as possible.'' ''Certainly,'' said Flynn, ''I'm going to Ostend.'' ''Good for you. Newspaper accounts shall be evidence; but send me the whole paper, and mark another passage, not the one referring to the bet.''

''O intellectual subtlety and stamina!''

''Have some more coffee?''

''Thanks.''

An hour later each, in his appointed lighthouse, was indicating the sure path of virtue and justice to the admiring English.

## II

The Trinity sittings were over. Sir Richard Ffoulkes – for the king's birthday had not left him without honor – was contemplating his wig and gown with disgust. On the table before him was a large leather book, containing many colored flies; and he had just assured himself that his seventeen-foot split cane was in good order. In fact, he had been boyish enough to test the check on his Hardy reel by practicing casts out of the window, to the alarm of the sparrows. It was the common routine for him on the brink of a holiday, but it never lost its freshness.

Then there came back to him the realization that this was to be no ordinary holiday. He was pledged to do murder.

He went over to the mirror, and studied his face steadily. He was perfectly calm; no trace of excitement showed in his keen features. ''I have always thought,'' he mused, ''That the crises of life are usually determined by accident. It is not possible to foresee events with mathematical accuracy, and in big things it is the small things that count. Hence the cleverest criminal may always make some slip, and the clumsiest escape by a piece of luck. Let me never forget the story of the officer at Gibraltar who, focussing a new field-glass, chanced to pick up a shepherd in the very act of crime. On the other hand, how many men have got clear away through stupid people disturbing or destroying the clues: from Jack the Ripper downwards! But it is the motive that counts. Where that does not exist, the strongest clues lead nowhere. For our surest faith is that men's actions are founded upon reason or upon desire. Hence the utter impossibility of guarding against lunatics or anarchists. I should hardly believe the evidence of my senses in such a case as this: Suppose the Master of the Rolls dropped in to see me, and in the course of a perfectly sound conversation, broke up my fishing-rod without explanation or apology, and, when questioned, calmly denied that he had done so. Who would believe my story? Hence I think that I could walk into the Strand, shoot a perfect stranger in the crowd, and throw away the gun, with no danger of being caught, provided only that the gun could not be traced to me. The evidence of those who saw me fire would be torn to pieces in cross-examination; they could even be made to disbelieve their own eyes.

''From this I draw these conclusions as to the proper conditions for my murder: First, there must be no conceivable reason for the act; second, there must be no way of tracing the weapon to my possession. I need not trouble to hide my traces, except in obvious matters like blood; for it is exceedingly stupid to attempt to prove a false alibi. In fact, there is no bigger booby-trap for a criminal, *pace* the indignant ghost of Mr. Weller, Senior.

''My plan is therefore a simple one; I have only to get hold of a weapon without detection, and use it upon an inoffensive stranger at any time when there happens to be nobody looking – though this is not so important.''

He returned to his fishing tackle. ''It's rather a big bet, though,'' he added; ''there's more than a thousand pounds to it. I think I will be pretty careful over details. Practice may not be quite so simple as theory!''

However, the first part of his programme turned out to be delightfully easy. It was his custom to train during the holiday by taking long walks, on his way to the lake or river where he fished. He detested motor-cars. As luck would have it, during the first week, as he tramped a lonely road, his eye was caught by an object lying on the ground. It was a heavy motor spanner, evidently left behind by some chauffeur who had had a breakdown. His mind instantly grasped the situation. There was no one in sight. The spanner was already rusted, had lain there some days. Any of a hundred people might have picked it up. It could never be traced to him. He had never possessed such a tool in his life; besides, the pattern was common. He thrust it quickly into his pocket. When he got home, he packed it away carefully in his travelling cashbox, a solid steel affair of which there was but one key, which never left his chain. ''Now,'' said he, ''the problem is to find the inoffensive stranger. I had better leave Scotland. Every one in Scotland is offensive. Also, in the matter of motive, our common humanity urges us all to kill Scotchmen. So goodbye, land o'cakes!''

Further meditations were in this key following: since he was to kill with the spanner, certain precautions must be taken. It must be a very clean kill, with no outcry or struggle. At the end of his cogitations, he decided that the victim had better be asleep. His legally trained mind had snapped its last link with the idea of adventure or sport;

his motto was "safety first." His attitude to his projected crime was simply that of preparing a brief; he wished to meet every contingency; the atrocity of his proceedings was invisible to his intellectuality. Reason is perfectly amoral.

It was on his way from Edinburgh to London that the brilliant idea occurred to him. He would kill old Miss Marsden! She was now Mrs. Robinson, by the way, for she had testified to the faith that was in her by marrying her protégé directly after his acquittal. Ffoulkes knew the house well; he had stayed there several days while working up the case. It was a lonely place, and the old lady was a fresh-air fiend, and slept on the veranda, winter and summer. She was perfectly friendly, had paid most liberally for the defense. Everything was in his favor. Even if Ezra happened to see the murder committed, his tongue was tied; indeed, he stood the strongest chance of being arrested for it himself. The servants slept far away from the veranda, at the other end of the old rambling house; there were no neighbors, and no dogs. His presence in the vicinity would excite no remark, for there was good dry-fly fishing in the streams. He would rent a cottage in the district for the second half of his holiday, walk over the downs, five miles or so, nothing to him, one moonless night, do the job, and walk back. A thousand to one that no one would know that he had ever left his cottage.

On this plan he acted. The only additional precautions suggested themselves to him on the spot; he cultivated the vicar assiduously, playing chess with him every evening; and he feigned a considerable devotion to that worthy gentleman's only daughter. It will be well, he thought, to seem to have my mind well occupied with the pleasures of a simpler chase. Further, the villagers would see nothing in a lover taking long walks by nights, in case he were seen leaving the cottage or returning to it.

A last refinement shot across his mental horizon when he began to calculate the time of the new moon. She would be just a week old on the anniversary of the Marsden murder. That would be the night for the job; the clever-clever novelist-detectives would fabricate a mystery of revenge in connection with the date. Ezra, too, would be away to meet Maud. There was, of course, a possibility that poignancy of memory would keep the old lady awake on that particular night; but he must chance that.

Things turned out for him even better than he had hoped. Three nights before the proposed crime the vicar mentioned casually that he had met young Robinson – "the charming lad whom you defended so brilliantly" – motoring to London – called away suddenly on business. He expected to be back in a week or ten days. No, Mrs. Robinson was not with him; "she is slightly ailing, poor lady, it appears."

When the great night came Ffoulkes made his masterstroke by proposing to the vicar's daughter. He was obviously accepted, and the young people, after dinner, went gaily arm-in-arm through the village, and received the congratulations of the few belated travelers in that early-to-bed-and-early-to-rise corner of the planet. But Ffoulkes had the spanner in his pocket, and after bestowing his fiancée at the vicarage, went, deviously at first, then swiftly and directly, over the downs. Luck followed him to the last; he found his victim fast asleep. A single blow of the spanner, which he had wrapped in a paper bag to deaden the sound, smashed in the skull; he made his way home without being seen or heard by anybody.

Two days later he wrote to Flynn, with a cutting from the local paper.

"My dear Jack, here's a terrible sequel to the Marsden murder. It is now clear that there is some family feud connected with the fatal date. Probably an affair going back a generation. Shocking, indeed, even to a hardened lawyer like myself; but you see how right I was to insist that there must have been a strong motive for Marsden's murder. Shall we ever know the truth? It sounds like an Arabian Nights' tale."

A month later he returned to London; he had had no answer from Flynn, and supposed him to be still away on his holiday.

There were no arrests, and no clues, in the matter of Mrs. Robinson. The spanner, which Ffoulkes had dropped by the veranda, served merely to suggest a tramp, who might conceivably have been a chauffeur gone to the bad. But the mystery was deepened by an amazing development; her husband had disappeared completely. There was no question of his complicity in the crime; for on the previous evening he had dined with the British Vice-Consul in Marseilles; and it was physically impossible for him to have returned in time to commit the murder.

The obvious deduction was that whoever hated the Marsdens had included him in the schedule.

"Well," soliloquized Ffoulkes in his chamber, "at least I shall not lose that thousand pounds. But now I've got to edge away from Miss Bread-and-Butter-and-Kisses. Ugh!"

III

When you have dined at Basso's, which is the summit of human felicity, you should avoid too sharp a declension to this vale of tears by taking a stroll along the quays to the old quarter on the west of the Bassin. There you will find streets almost worthy to rank with the Fishmarket at Cairo, and decidedly superior to even the best that Hong Kong or Honolulu or New Orleans can produce. In particular, there is an archway called by initiates the Gate of Hell, for it forms an entrance to this highly fascinating and exceedingly disreputable district.

Under this archway, on the night of the exploit of Sir Richard Ffoulkes, stood a young man, quietly dressed in the English style, though with a trifling tendency to overindulgence in jewelry.

He glanced at a watch upon his wrist; ten minutes before midnight. He then took a little bottle from his pocket, after a quick inspection of the vicinity. From the bottle he shook a few grains of powder on the back of his hand, and drew them into his nostrils. Next came a moment's indecision; then, swinging his cane, he walked briskly out of the archway, and paced up and down a strange little square of green, set there as if somehow hallowed by great memories. After a little while he returned to the archway. This time it was tenanted. A girl stood there. She was dressed in plain black with the extreme of modesty and refinement; but the piquancy and vitality of her face, and the lustre and passion of her eyes, redeemed the picture from banality.

There was a long look of recognition; the girl reached out both arms. The man took them in his own. For a minute they stood, feeding on each other, prolonging the delicious torture of restraint. Then slowly they drew together, and their mouths met in an abandoned kiss.

It would have puzzled them to say how long the embrace lasted; but at its truce they saw that they were not alone. Close to them stood another man, tall, elegant, slim, almost feminine in figure, as he certainly was in the extremity of the fashion which tailored him. Nor was there wanting a touch of rouge and powder on his cheeks. His thin, white hand was lifted to his nostrils, and the lovers perceived that he was taking advantage of the darkness to indulge in cocaine.

The newcomer spoke in silken tones. "Forgive me," he said in softest French, "but it gave me pleasure to be near you. I saw monsieur here a few moments ago, and knew that he was one of the elect. And mademoiselle, too? May I have the honor?"

The girl smiled. "Among friends," she murmured charmingly, and raised the back of her hand towards him. He saluted it with his lips, and then shook out a generous supply of crystal poison from a snuff-box in amber and emeralds that dated from the great days of Louis XIV.

The girl turned her eyes full upon him, almost ardently. "I haven't touched it," she said, "for ever so long. By the way, excuse me, won't you, but aren't we all English?"

"I am," said the exquisite. "I'm an actor on a holiday. Won't you come to my rooms? It's only a garret, or little better, but I have plenty of the Snow of Heaven, and we could have a wonderful night." "Let's go!" said the girl, pressing her lover's arm. He hesitated a moment. "Three's company," urged the other, "when they all understand."

"It would be perfect," chimed the girl, "and it would suit us – in other ways," she added, darkly. "Yes, the scheme has points," admitted the younger man: "thanks very much. We'll come. What's your name? Mine's Herbert Aynes. This lady – we'll call her Mab, if you don't mind. There's an injured husband in the offing, you know: that's one reason why we have to be careful." "Certainly, prudence before all things; but I've no troubles; call me Francis Ridley." They linked arms, and strolled gaily along the main street of the quarter, enchanted by the color and the chiaroscuro, by the hoarse cries in all strange tongues that greeted them on every side, even by the weird odors – for when people are lit by love and adventure and cocaine, there is no place of this whole universe which is not sheer delight. Presently, however, they branched off, under Ridley's direction, and began to climb the steep streets on their right. A minute later they entered an ancient doorway, and after three flights of stairs found Ridley's dovecote.

It was a charming room, furnished, as if for a woman, with all bright colors and daintiness. On one side of the room was a divan, smothered in cushions; on the other a hammock of scarlet cords hung from the rafters. Ridley went to the window and closed the shutters. "Madame est chez elle!" he announced gallantly. "What a wonder-

ful place!" laughed the girl. "However did you find it?"

"Oh, it used to be a house of assignation."

"Used to be!"

And this time all three laughed in unison.

## IV

The reopening of the courts found Ffoulkes enormously preoccupied. For the past two years several influential newspapers had been accusing Ministers of the Crown of the grossest kind of robbery. They had bought and sold stock, it was alleged, manipulating the prices by using their positions to announce that the government had or had not decided to make contracts with the companies involved, and subsequently denying the rumors when they had taken their profits. The attack had been so persistent that the accused ministers had been forced to desperate measures. They had started a prearranged libel action against a newspaper in Paris for reprinting one of these articles; but people still asked why they did not prosecute one of the sheets that were attacking them in London. Unhappily, not one of these was to be bought: each, carefully sounded, announced its intention to fight; and redoubled its venom.

It was at last decided to attempt a criminal prosecution of the weakest of its enemies, a paper edited by a man personally unpopular, and to bring every kind of indirect pressure upon the court to secure a conviction.

Of course the law officers of the Crown were unavailable for the prosecution; and the choice of a leader had fallen, at the last moment, when their own counsel suddenly declined to go on with the case and returned the briefs, upon Ffoulkes.

He had thus only a month to assimilate what really required six; but if he won, he could be sure of office next time a Liberal Government was in power.

So he worked day and night, seeing nobody but the solicitors and witnesses employed on the case.

He had no news of Flynn but a telegram from Berlin, saying that he would be back in a month, and that there was "nothing to report as yet." This amused Ffoulkes hugely; it would be great if Flynn failed to bring off his murder. However, he had no time for trifles like murder these days: he had to get a conviction for criminal libel; nothing else mattered.

But when the case came actually into court he saw it to be hopeless. His opening was masterly: it occupied two days; but on the second day he sent word to his clients during the lunch hour that it was no good to go on, and that he felt forced to take measures previously agreed upon. These were simple; near the conclusion of the speech he managed to blunder into disclosing a flaw in the procedure so obvious that the judge could not possibly overlook it. His lordship interrupted: "I am afraid, Sir Richard, that you have no case. If you will refer to Jones vs. The Looking Glass, you will see that it has been expressly laid down that –" An elaborate legal argument followed, but the judge was inexorable. "You must redraw your plea, Sir Richard. The case is dismissed."

The docile organs of the government condoled with the great counsel for losing an "already won case" on a technicality; but Ffoulkes was sorry he had ever touched it. He would go to the club and play a game of chess. Flynn would be there later; he had returned to London that morning, and telegraphed his friend to make it a dinner and the Empire.

In the lounge of the club was only one little old man, who was known as a mathematician of great eminence, with a touch of the crank. He had recently finished a pamphlet to prove that the ancients had some knowledge of fourth-dimensional mathematics, that their statement of such problems as the duplication of the cube implied an apprehension of some medium in which incommensurables became tractable. He was especially strong on Euclid's parallel postulate, which has not only been unproved, but proved unprovable. He was also a deep student of Freemasonry, whose arcana furnished him with further arguments on the same thesis.

This old man, whose name was Simon Iff, challenged Ffoulkes to a game of chess. To the surprise of the lawyer, who was a very strong amateur, he was beaten thrice in very short games. Iff then took off a knight, and won a fourth game as easily as before. "It's no good, sir," said Ffoulkes; "I see you are in the master class." "Not a bit of it," replied the old man, "Lasker can beat me as easily as I beat you. He really knows chess; I only know you. I can gauge your intellect; it is limited in certain directions. I had a lost game against you most of the time; but you did not make the winning continuations, and I knew that you wouldn't and couldn't.

"Let me tell you something, if you'll forgive a senior for prosing. There are two ways to play chess. One is a man against a man; the other is a man against a chess-board. It's the difference between match and medal play at golf. Observe; if I know that you are going to play the Philidor defense to the King's Knight's Opening, I do not risk being forced into the Petroff, which I dislike. But in playing an unknown quantity, I must analyze every position like a problem, and guard against all possibilities. It takes a great genius and a lifetime's devotion to play the latter game. But so long as I can read your motive in a move, so long as I can content myself with guarding that one line. Should you make a move whose object I cannot see, I am compelled to take a fresh view of the board, and analyze the position as if I were called upon to adjudicate an unfinished game."

"That's exceedingly interesting. It bears rather on my game, law."

"I was about to venture a remark upon that point. I was fortunate enough to be present at the trial of Ezra Robinson, and I cannot compliment you too highly on the excellence of your defense. But, as you will be the first to admit, his acquittal was no solution of the question. 'Who killed Marsden?' Still less does it tell us who killed Mrs. Robinson exactly one year later."

"Do you know the solution?"

"No; but I can show you on what lines to attack the mystery."

"I wish you would."

"I may be tedious."

"Impossible. You have beaten me so abominably at chess that I am all on fire to learn more from watching the working of your intellect."

"Intellect is our weakest weapon. This world is run upon 'inflexible intellectual guiders,' as Zoroaster put it, but it was 'the will of the Father,' as he also explained, which laid down those laws which we call laws of nature, but, as Kant has shown, are really no more than the laws of our own minds. The universe is a phenomenon of love under will, a mystic and poetic creation, and the intellect only stands to it as mere scansion does to poetry."

"It is at least a charming theory."

"It works, Sir Richard. Let us apply our frail powers to this Marsden mystery. Let us take the second murder first, because it is apparently the more abstruse. We have no clues and no motives to mislead us. True, Robinson had a strong interest in his wife's death—yet not only does he prove an alibi, but he vanishes forever! If, as we might imagine, he had hired a knave to do the job, he would have kept in sight, pretended decent grief, and so on. Of course, as has been suggested, he may himself have come to some sudden end; but if that be so, it is a marvelous coincidence indeed. No! We are forced to believe him guiltless, of this second murder at least. Consequently, having eliminated the only person with a motive, we are thrown back upon the master's way of playing chess, pure analysis. (Notice how Tchigorin handicapped himself by his fancy for that second move, queen to king's second, and Steinitz by his pawn to queen's third in the Ruy Lopez. Their opponents got a line on them at once, and saved themselves infinite trouble.) Pardon the digression. Now then, let us look at this second murder again. What is the most striking fact about it? This, that it was committed by a person with a complete contradiction in his mind. He is so astute that he leaves no clue of any sort; there has not even been any arrest. If he did the first murder also, it shows that he is capable of turning the same trick twice. In short, we see a man of the first-class mind, or rather intellect, for we must assume a lack of moral sense. A man, in fact, with a mind like your own; for since this afternoon's exploit, I imagine you will not claim to be scrupulous."

"You saw through the trick?"

"Naturally; you knew you had no case, so you preferred to lose on a foul, and claim a moral victory."

"Good for you!"

"Well, this same first-rate intellect is in another respect so feeble that the man takes pleasure, or finds satisfaction, in arranging his crime on a significant date. He must be the sort of man that takes precautions against witches on Walpurgis Night!"

"Jove, that's a good point. Never struck me!" "Well, frankly, it doesn't strike me now. There are men with such blind spots, no doubt; but it is easier for me to think that the murderer, with plenty of nights to choose from, chose that one in particular with the idea of leading people astray – of playing on their sense of romance and mystery – of exploiting their love of imaginative detective stories!"

"If so, the point is once more in favor of his intellect."

"Exactly. But now we are going to narrow the circle. Who is there in whose mind the date of the first murder was so vivid that such a stratagem would occur to him?"

"Well, there are many. Myself, for example!"

Iff began to set up the pieces for another game.

"We must eliminate you," he said, after a few moments of silence, "you lawyers forget your cases as soon as they are over."

"Besides, I had no possible motive."

"Oh, that is nothing in the case. You are a rich man, and would never do a murder for greed; you are a cold-blooded man, and would never kill for revenge or jealousy; and these things place you apart from the common run of men. Still, I believe such as you perfectly capable of murder; there are seven deadly sins, not two; why should you not kill, for example, from some motive like pride?"

"I take pride in aiding the administration of justice. My ambition is a Parliamentary career."

"Come," said Iff, "all this is a digression; we had better play chess. Let me try at Blackburne's odds!" Iff won the game. "You know," he said, as Ffoulkes overturned his king in sign of surrender, "whoever killed Mrs. Robinson, if I read his type of mind aright, has left his queen *en prise*, after all. There is a very nasty gap in the defenses. He killed the woman from no common motive; he has therefore always to be on his guard against equally uncommon men. Suppose Casablanca dropped into the club, and challenged me to a game, how should I feel if I had any pride in beating you? There may be some one hunting him who is as superior intellectually to him as he is to the police. And there's a worse threat: he probably took the precaution of killing the old woman in her sleep. He could have no conscience, no remorse. But he would have experience in his own person that such monsters as himself were at large; therefore, I ask you, how does he know, every night, that some one will not kill him in his sleep?"

Ffoulkes called the waiter, and asked Iff to join him in a drink. "No, thank you," returned the old man, "playing chess is the only type of pleasure I dare permit myself."

At this moment Flynn came into the club, and greeted both men warmly. Iff had written many a glowing essay for the Irishman's review. He wanted both to dine with him, but once again Iff declined, pleading another engagement. After a few moments' chat he walked off, leaving the two old friends together.

They dined at the club, and pointedly confined the conversation to the libel case, and politics in general. With their second cigars, Flynn rose. "Come round to Mount Street," he said. "I've a lot to tell you." So they strolled off in the bright autumn weather to the maisonette where Flynn lived.

## V

They made themselves at ease on the big Chesterfield. It was a strange room, a symphony of green. The walls were covered with panels of green silk; the floor was covered with great green carpet from Algeria; the upholstery was of green morocco; the ceiling was washed in delicate eau-de-Nil with designs by Gauguin, and the lamps were shaded by soft tissues of emerald. Even the drinks were of the same color: Chartreuse, the original shipping, and crème de menthe and absinthe. Flynn's man brought cigarettes and cigars in a box of malachite,

and set them down with the spirits. Flynn dismissed him for the night.

"Well," said Jack, when the man had gone, "I see you got away with it all right."

"I had a scare this afternoon. Old Iff made rings round me at chess, and then proceeded to develop a theory of the – exploit – that was so near the truth that I thought for half a moment that he had guessed something. Luckily, he's just an old crank in everybody's eyes; but, by Jove, he can play chess!"

"Iff's one of the biggest minds in England; but the second-raters always win in London."

"Well, what about your end of the bet?"

"Oh, there's no news yet. But they'll find the bodies next week when my tenancy of the place expires."

"Bodies!"

"Two. You see, I went after your friend Ezra Robinson and the fair Duval. I knew from you of the appointment on the anniversary of the murder, but not the place; so I had him shadowed from the day of the bet. I took a room in the old quarter of Marseilles, when I found that he had stopped there. I got myself up as Francis Ridley, whom you may remember in certain amateur theatricals.

"I got them along to make a night of it, and filled them up with cocaine, while I took – mostly borax. Then when we got to the stage of exhaustion and collapse, I unslung a convenient hammock that hung in the room and told them what I meant to do. And then I hanged them by the neck until they were dead, and may the Lord have mercy on their souls! Next day I crossed to Algiers, went down to El Kantara and shot moufflon – I'm having a fine head mounted especially for you – then I came back through Italy and Germany. That's all!"

"I say," cried Ffoulkes, shocked, "that's hardly in the spirit of the bet, old man. I don't see any moral turpitude involved!"

"You wretched hypocrite," retorted Flynn, "it was deliberate murder by both French and English law. I don't see what you can want more than that. You ought to be ashamed of yourself, with your legal mind!"

But the lawyer was not satisfied. He began to argue, and ultimately turned the discussion into what was as near a quarrel as such old friends could ever contemplate. In fact, Ffoulkes saw the danger, and went home at an unusually early hour.

Flynn dismissed the matter from his mind, and passed the night in composing sonnets, in French, to the honor of the green goddess – absinthe.

## VI

A month later. Flynn had been unusually busy, and saw little of his friends. Twice he dined with Ffoulkes, but the latter was more moody and irritable than ever. He had lost three important cases, and seemed altogether out of luck. His looks reflected his worry as much as his manners. Flynn asked him to come to Paris for a week's rest; he refused; Flynn went alone.

Returning to London, he called at the chambers in Lincoln's Inn. They were shut up. He went on to the club, hoping for news.

Almost the first man he saw was an old college friend, a judge, the very man to have the latest tidings. Probably Ffoulkes had been in court that day.

"Hush! it's terrible," said the judge, and drew Flynn into a corner of the lounge. "They had to take him away yesterday. He had persecution mania, a hopeless form, I'm afraid. Hadn't slept for a month. Said he was afraid of being murdered in his sleep! These things are too bad to talk about; I'm going home. Brace up!" The judge rose and went; but when Flynn came out of the stupor into which the intelligence had thrown him, he found Iff seated at his side.

"You've heard? Isn't it awful?"

"No," replied Iff, "not more so than the fact that two and two make four. Which in a sense is awful indeed, and according as you are for or against the tendency of the universe, is encouraging or terrifying. But it is fatal and inexorable. Perhaps to say that is to say enough!"

"Explain what you mean."

"A little while ago," replied the old mystic, "he came here to play chess with me – you remember; you were there, the day of your return. Well, I mastered his mind; I saw its limitations; I mapped its roads; I measured its heights and depths; I calculated its reactions. I beat him easily, at odds. We then began to talk of the Marsden mystery, and I analyzed the mind of the man who killed Mrs. Robinson – a mind like his own. I showed that the coincidence of dates was probably a deliberate false trail. I then asked who would be likely to think of such a point, who would have vivid reason to think of that date. I was speaking in perfectly general terms; no suspicion of him had crossed my mind. He instantly suggested himself. I knew how he played chess: so I knew that he must have had himself in view subconsciously; that he must be trying to put me off the scent by boldness. It was just the same type of tactics as choosing the anniversary of the first murder. From that instant I knew that he was guilty.

"A moment later he confirmed me. I suggested that a man like himself might kill for such a motive as pride; and he replied that he took pride in the administration of justice. Now after that libel action, and coming from such a man, the English hypocrisy, which might have been natural in a lesser man, was a complete confession. Therefore I determined to punish him. I knew there was only one way; to work upon his mind along its own lines. So I said to him: "Suppose the murderer realizes that there are intellects superior to his own? And – how will he sleep, knowing that there are people who will murder others in their sleep without reasonable cause? You know the answer. I suppose that I am in a sense the murderer of his reason."

Flynn said nothing; but his eyes were streaming; he had loved Dick Ffoulkes dearly, and a thousand memories were urgent in his heart and mind. Iff seemed not to notice it.

"But the murderer of Marsden is still a mystery. Ffoulkes can hardly have done that."

Flynn sat up and laughed wildly. "I'll tell you all about that," he cried. "Ezra Robinson did it, with the help of the floor clerk. They were to meet on the anniversary of the murder. I tracked them down, and I hanged them with these hands." He stretched them out in a gesture of agony. The old man took them in his.

"Boy!" he said, " – for you will never grow up – you have perhaps erred in some ways–ways which I find excusable – but you need never lose a night's sleep over this business."

"Ah!" cried Jack, "but it was I who tempted my friend – it was a moment of absolute madness, and now I have lost him!"

"We are all punished," said the old man solemnly, "exactly where we have offended, and in the measure thereof."

# Crowley Today

We are in the midst of an occult revival. The name of Aleister Crowley once again looms large, as a multiplicity of magical fraternities claim him as spiritual forefather: most confusing for the uninitiated is the way in which the title of 'Ordo Templi Orientis' has been claimed by several conflicting organisations in recent years, each placing their own interpretation on Crowley's wishes.

There have been three main OTO claimants: Marcelo Ramos Motta (a Brazilian whose Tennessee-based version tended to a rather pompous, authoritarian style, issuing insulting statements about other claimants); the late Grady Louis McMurtry (a much-respected former USA army major); and Kenneth Grant (an ex-student of Crowley and well-known occult author). The situation was made a little clearer when, in 1985, an American court essentially put Motta out of the running by finding in favour of McMurtry's 'Caliphate' OTO. Sadly, McMurtry died before hearing of the decision. The case was between Motta and McMurtry and did not involve Grant, who continues to run an OTO in the UK with no apparent authority other than the fact that he desires to do so. He is, however, a worthy occultist doing interesting research, and seems to be on good terms with the Caliphate.

Crowley's influence extends further than the OTO, however. It was at one time evident in the Church of Satan, for example, which was run by that unusual San Francisco showman Anton Szandor LaVey until a mass-defection in 1975. LaVey, author of *The Satanic Bible* and *The Satanic Rituals*, perhaps took his emulation of Crowley *too* far when he tried the Crowleyan tactic of milking the gullible by asking devotees to pay heavily for enlightenment (or so the story goes). His disciple Michael Aquino now runs a new organisation, The Temple of Set, along rather more ascetic and intellectual lines. There is evidence that Charles Manson, leader of the infamous kill-crazy desert cult implicated in the Sharon Tate murders, may have been involved with the somewhat disreputable OTO

# PSYCHIC T.V.

*Left*: Collage from limited-edition record package by Psychic T.V., performance arm of the Temple Ov Psychick Youth.
*Opposite*: Psychick Youth bulletin.

branch run by one Jean Brayton in late-60s California. Details of the activities of Brayton can be found in Ed Sanders's book on Manson, *The Family*, although it would be grossly unfair to blame Crowley for these perversions of his magickal ideas.

One of the most intriguing Crowley-inspired cults today is The Temple Ov Psychick Youth, a movement dreamed up by former UK performance artist Genesis P-Orridge and incorporating concepts from the work of William Burroughs and Brion Gysin alongside magick and ritual culled from a variety of sources. The members dress in uniform yet promote individualism; they use ritual but are interested in the chaos of violence. It would take a whole book to examine a non-religion which markets videos of the Jim Jones massacre in Guyana and nevertheless is essentially life-promoting, but some of the Temple's Crowley-inspired material is reproduced here.

*Left*: Letter from Crowley's friend Grady McMurtry (late head of the OTO) to rock star and Crowleyana collector, Jimmy Page.

**All religious groups, cults and societies develop a conscious boundary between those who have membership and those who do not**

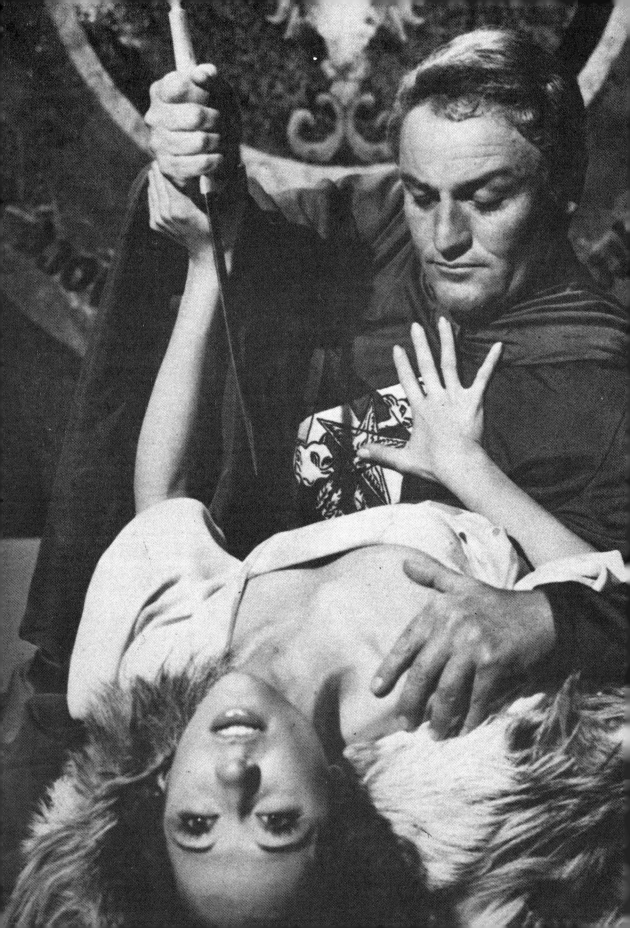

# Crowley on Film

It's odd that the only mainstream movie based on Crowley to date appears to be the extremely rare Rex Ingram silent *The Magician* (1926), a film involving the talents of Michael Powell and based on Somerset Maugham's book of the same title. At the moment, however, there are at least two features and a documentary about Crowley in pre-production, though given the fate of past scripts on his legend it would be pointless to speculate on whether the movies will ever see the light of day. Prime contender could be Snoo Wilson's version of his stage play, *The Beast*.

The smoothly sinister Charles Gray has played two Crowleyan villains: the depraved Mocata, in the film of Dennis Wheatley's *The Devil Rides Out* (1968), and murderous demonologist Bellow in TV's *Bergerac* series. But Crowley-based film villains are few and far between, though Niall McGinnis was an effective Karswell in *Night Of The Demon* (1957), based on M. R. James's *Casting The Runes*.

So far it is the experimental film which has explored the Crowley legacy: a bizarre film called *Decoder* (1984) was made in Germany starring William Burroughs, the *avant-garde* writer, and the release was accompanied by a book containing various explanatory pieces, including a pirated translation of one of my own Crowley articles from a UK magazine. The main Crowleyan film-maker today, however, is Kenneth Anger.

Anger began his movie career as a child actor in 1935 in the Hollywood version of *A Midsummer Night's Dream*, and later gained notoriety with his two *Hollywood Babylon* books, filled with scurrilous anecdotes concerning the sex and drug thrills of movieland's big names. A serious student of magick, his own films have varied from homosexual fantasies about leather (*Scorpio Rising*, 1963) and sailors (*Fireworks*, 1947) to the area of gloriously ecstatic Crowleyan ritual, such as *Inauguration Of The Pleasure Dome* (1954).

Anger has often revised and updated his movies, adding

*Left*: Oliver Haddo (Paul Wegner) is the Crowleyan figure in Rex Ingram's 1927 film *The Magician*.

*Above*: Marjorie Cameron in Kenneth Anger's *Inauguration of the Pleasure Dome*.

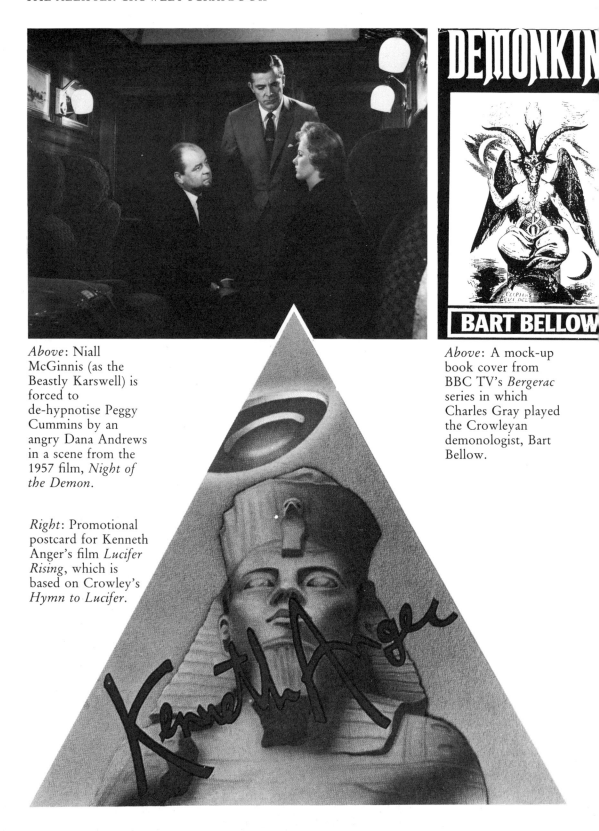

*Above*: Niall McGinnis (as the Beastly Karswell) is forced to de-hypnotise Peggy Cummins by an angry Dana Andrews in a scene from the 1957 film, *Night of the Demon*.

*Right*: Promotional postcard for Kenneth Anger's film *Lucifer Rising*, which is based on Crowley's *Hymn to Lucifer*.

*Above*: A mock-up book cover from BBC TV's *Bergerac* series in which Charles Gray played the Crowleyan demonologist, Bart Bellow.

DEMONKIN

BART BELLOW

soundtracks by famous rock stars to some: *Invocation Of My Demon Brother (Arrangement In Black & Gold)* (1969) features a synthesiser soundtrack by Mick Jagger, while one version of the above mentioned *Pleasure Dome* film uses the music of ELO. Anger's most notorious film, though, is his long-term project *Lucifer Rising* (1970–80).

This film is worth a book in itself: much of the original footage was stolen by Bobby Beausoleil, a member of the infamous Manson 'Family' and the choice at one point to play Lucifer, who buried it in the Californian desert! Later on, Anger got Jimmy Page of Led Zeppelin (himself a Crowley fan) to write soundtrack music, but they fell out and Anger is said to have ritually cursed Page! The film as it stands now has a new soundtrack recorded by Beausoleil in prison while serving time for murdering music teacher Gary Hinman on the (supposed) orders of Charles Manson.

*Lucifer Rising*, like all things Crowleyan, seems tinged with both greatness and madness.

*Below*: Drawing and page of film script by Deirdre Anne Le Blanc, based on Jean Overton Fuller's book *The Magical Dilemma of Victor Neuberg*.

Aleister Crowley

# Flexipop!

No. 666
65p

## RETURN OF *the* BEAST

### Aleister Crowley — Pop Guru

plus: **DAVID BOWIE**
XMAL DEUTSCHLAND,
**ABBO** FLESH FOR LULU,
LYDIA LUNCH, **PAUL YOUNG**
KIM WILDE, **BOW WOW WOW**

# The Crowley Industry: Rock and Beyond

*Opposite*: The last issue of the rockzine *Flexipop* boasted an article by David Tibet (member of occult band Current 93) on the influence of Crowley on popular music.

As mentioned in the introduction, Aleister Crowley continues to exert a profound fascination, not least on the rock stars who can afford to indulge themselves in his style.

The Beatles included him on the sleeve of their legendary album *Sgt Pepper's Lonely Hearts Club Band* (1967). Both Anton La Vey and Kenneth Anger claim to have inspired the song 'Sympathy For The Devil' by The Rolling Stones, but Crowley may be the true key to their obsessions, especially as exemplified by the LP *Their Satanic Majesties Request* (1967)!

Of course, the 60's were littered with magickal casualties: jazz/rocker Graham Bond thought he was Crowley's illegitimate son and died under a tube train in mysterious circumstances. His music was heavily influenced by the Beast's ideas.

These days the Crowley influence seems split into two streams as far as pop/rock is concerned. Firstly there is the hard-rock and heavy-metal genre: groups like Venom, Witchfynde, Iron Maiden and so on ramble incoherently about the occult in their lyrics, while the record covers are littered with inverted crucifixes and rotting zombies. If the best is Ozzy Osbourne yowling about 'Mr Crowley', you can imagine what the worst sounds like. For the most part these groups have no real knowledge of Crowley's ideas and are only interested in sensationalism and selling vinyl.

The other type of Crowley-band tends to be doomy and pseudo-'Gothic', like the (hopefully) defunct Blood & Roses, who boasted a black-clad girl vocalist nasally crooning about 'doing what thou wilt'. The fact is that the worthwhile mentions of Crowley in rock have, quite naturally, come from individualists.

David Bowie sang about being *'closer to the Golden Dawn/ immersed in Crowley's uniform of imagery'* on the song 'Quicksand' from his 1971 album *Hunky Dory*. The approach is neither vulgar nor exploitative. The most famous rock Crowleyan is obviously Jimmy Page, formerly of Led Zeppelin (*not* a heavy-metal band – *listen*) who had the words 'Do What Thou Wilt' unobtrusively engraved on the

seldiy bate and nigel bourne
PAGAN EASTER

RITUAL MUSIC FOR TH

*Opposite*: This LP and single indicate the sadly unimaginative way in which the Great Beast's image is often used by rock groups today.

*Above*: An album of Equinox music issued under the aegis of the Crowleyan Temple Ov Psychick Youth.

*Right*: 'Immersed in Crowley's uniform'? David Bowie may wear a crucifix today, but he was once deeply involved in the occult and mentioned Crowley in the song *Quicksand*.

Do what thou wilt shall be the whole of the Law.

# LED ZEPPELIN

## JIMMY PAGE DISCIPLE OF ALEISTER CROWLEY

O.T.O.

△ JIMMY PAGE STUDIED CROWLEYS MAGICKAL WRITINGS AS A SCHOOL BOY. △ AT ONE TIME OWNED THE EQUINOX BOOKSHOP IN LONDON, SPECIALIZING IN RARE CROWLEY BOOKS. △ OWNS AND IS RESTORING, CROWLEY'S, FORMER TEMPLE/HOME BOLESKINE HOUSE, ON THE LOCKNESS. △ PAGE OWNS THE SECOND LARGEST CROWLEY BOOK COLLECTION IN THE WORLD. △ CROWLEYS THELEMAIC MOTTO "DO WHAT THOU WILT" IS ENGRAVED ON PAGES LED ZEPPELIN III LP. △ PAGES HERMIT SCENE IN THE L.Z. FILM, SONG REMAINS THE SAME WAS SHOT AT BOLESKINE. PAGE COM~ POSED & RECORDED THE SOUNDTRACK FOR KENNETH ANGERS CROWLEYIAN FILM, LUCIFER RISING, & APPEARS SUBLIMINALY IN THE FILM, HOLDING THE STELE OF REVEALING, STAREING AT CROWLEY'S PHOTO. For more information on Page or Crowleys Secret Magickal Order the O.T.O. Write : BOLESKINE O.T.O. P.O. BOX 94 CARMICHAEL, CALIFORNIA, 95608.

Details $1.                    Love is the law, love under will.

*Above*: Promo flyer for the album of Jimmy Page's discarded soundtrack for Kenneth Anger's Crowleyan movie *Lucifer Rising*.

*Opposite*: Advert for the Page soundtrack to *Lucifer Rising*.

# KENNETH ANGER'S
# LUCIFER RISING
## UNLEASHED IN THE WEST

# JIMMY PAGE
## SOUNDTRACK

12 IN. Stereo E.P.  Pressed on Quality Vinyl    Extended Play 23 Minutes

**1000 Numbered First Editions Unleashed**

### B/W FRONT COVER

Blow-Up Lucifer Rising frame of Jimmy Page
holding the Stèle of Revealing (718) while
gazing at Aleister Crowley's wreathed photo.

### B/W BACK COVER

A Gallery of rare Jimmy Page, Aleister Crowley,
Boleskine House, Equinox Bookstore, and
Lucifer Rising Stills.

Money Orders Only, Payable to:

Boleskine House Records

P.O. Box 94, Carmichael,
California 95608 U.S.A.

INCLUDE:

# $19.95

$4.00 For Postage & Handling
$1.00 For each additional album

LIBER AL vel LEGIS CH.2 VS.78

## SECURE A NUMBERED EDITION, ORDER ASAP!

FRATER ZARDOZ IV P.I. BOLESKINE O.T.O.

# THE BOLESKINE O.T.C
## PRESENTS THE PREMIERE OF
# LUCIFER RISING

THE KENNETH ANGER FILM · MUSIC BY BOBBY BEAUSOLEIL AND THE FREEDOM ORCHESTRA

**FRI.
OCT.
23
MID-
$4.00**

**FRI.
OCT.
23
NITE
$4.00**

# SHOWCASE CINEMA
KENNETH ANGER IN PERSON      412 L ST SACTO, CA.
MAGICK LANTERN CYCLE•THE COMPLETE FILMS OF KENNETH ANGER

*Opposite*: Letter from Kenneth Anger, written on the flyer for the final soundtrack of *Lucifer Rising* by convicted murderer Bobby Beausoleil. The poster advertising its screening (*above*) is by celebrated rock album cover artist Rick Griffin.

*Opposite*:
Mock-satanic
contract by
underground
cartoonist and occult
book collector Savage
Pencil, who is
planning a possible
comic adaptation of
Crowley's
pornographic *White
Stains*!

run-off of their third album. Page has a truly magnificent
collection of Crowleyana, including books, manuscripts,
robes, and even Boleskine House, the Beast's Highland
home. He used to run a Crowley bookshop/publishing con-
cern called *Equinox*, and – as mentioned earlier – composed
soundtrack material for an early version of Kenneth Anger's
film *Lucifer Rising* before falling out with the film-maker. An
album of that music was recently issued in America, but it
has resulted in the man behind the project (Chris Dietler)
being expelled from the OTO for 'pirating' the material. Dietler
claims to have had permission from Anger but Page seems not
to have been consulted. Nevertheless – acrimony notwith-
standing – the music is haunting stuff, certainly worth hearing.

Genesis P-Orridge's band Psychic TV are a musical art
platform for a Crowleyan cult called The Temple Ov Psychick Youth, mentioned earlier. And again the occult jinx
creeps in – several of the best experimental groups around
have worked in the past with P-Orridge but seem anxious to
avoid being connected with his ideas.

Coil are one such outfit, using scatalogical themes and
imagery in pursuit of their magickal ideals, which lean towards
the homosexual end of Crowleyana. Another is David Tibet's
Current 93, a real Crowley cult band if ever there was one.

Perhaps we've come full circle with the recent issue of an
LP by Crowley himself, of cleaned-up wax-cylinder record-
ings of him reading poetry and magickal invocations.

*Below*: Crowley's
exploits, as depicted
in *Occult Laff Parade*
comic book. Art by
Kim Deitch.

# ALEISTER CROWLEY'S

# RITES OF ELEUSIS

| | | |
|---|---|---|
| THE RITE OF SATURN | Aug. 30 | 10 P.M. |
| THE RITE OF JUPITER | Sept. 5 | NOON |
| THE RITE OF MARS | Sept. 10 | 8 P.M. |
| THE RITE OF SOL | Sept. 15 | NOON |
| THE RITE OF VENUS | Sept. 20 | 7 P.M. |
| THE RITE OF MERCURY | Sept. 25 | 8 P.M. |
| THE RITE OF LUNA | Sept. 30 | 8 P.M. |

## 5205 RAILROAD AVE.  PITTSBURG, CA.

Call: 415 439-9794/222-7393

*Above*: Flyer for modern re-enactment of Rites of Eleusis.

*Opposite*: Dust-wrapper and rare promotional band on a first edition of John Symonds's classic biography *The Great Beast*.

# Bibliography

To list all the books by and about Aleister Crowley would serve little purpose here – indeed, it would fill a volume in itself. What follows, then, is simply a suggested reading list for the novice who wants to learn more about Crowley and the areas covered in the present tome.

*The Great Beast* by John Symonds (Macdonald 1971)
The best of the biographies; this is an updated version containing material from another Symonds effort, *The Magic Of Aleister Crowley*. The rumour is that a new, even more updated reprint is planned.

*The Confessions Of Aleister Crowley* (Routledge & Kegan Paul 1979 – corrected edn)
Complete text of all six volumes, shorn of waffle and edited by Symonds and Kenneth Grant. The original edition by Mandrake Press was only at proof stage of book three when the firm went bankrupt.

*Magick In Theory & Practice* by Aleister Crowley (Dover)
His *magnum opus*.

*The Books Of The Beast* by Timothy d'Arch Smith (Aquarian)
Occult essays by a master researcher. The first sheds light on Crowley's publishing methods.

*White Stains* by Aleister Crowley (Duckworth)
Reissue of his notorious pornographic work.

*The Rebirth Of Magic* by Francis King & Isabel Sutherland (Corgi)
Useful history of the Golden Dawn *et al*.

The situation regarding Crowley's poetry is vexed; there is only one recent volume suitable for the general reader, Martin Booth's *Aleister Crowley* from Aquarian. For fictional representations one need look no further than the chart printed earlier in this book: everything on it is worth reading. There is much on the Lovecraft/Crowley connection; the trouble is that the best of it (Kenneth Grant's series of books for Muller) is too complex for the novice, while the rest tends towards the puerile.

For those interested in rock music and Crowley there is little available, though (if I may be permitted a plug) 1988 will see the publication of my own book on occultism and popular music/culture, *Rock Magick*.

A final literary note: it's a little-known fact that Aleister Crowley once railed against the publishers of this fine volume because they'd issued a work by his hated rival A.E. Waite, calling the firm "a Foul – Sham"! How wrong could he be . . .

## Acknowledgements

It's impossible to name everyone who helped with this book, but it'd certainly be a lesser effort were it not for the following: Barry Belasco at Foulsham; Lynne Nazareth, my Editor, and Tony Truscott, Designer; Edwin Pouncey; Phil Nutman of *Fangoria* magazine; N. Oddie; Francis King; Peter Brogan of Hulton Picture Library; Judith at Rough Trade; David Tibet; Clive Harper; Deirdre Anne Le Blanc; photographer Tony Mottram; David Rietti of the OTO; Victor Hall of Victim Press; Colin Wilson; Genesis P-Orridge; Atlantis Bookshop; John Balance and Peter Christopherson of Coil; Timothy d'Arch Smith; the Estate of Beresford Egan; Chris Dietler; Colindale Newspaper Library. Sincere apologies for any omissions.

**Picture credits**
**BBC Hulton Picture Library**: p 6, 10, 12, 13, 14, 16, 17, 22, 26, 28, 32, 38, 40, 41, 42, 43, 44, 45, 46, 47, 48, 50, 51, 53 (left), 56, 57, 58, 59, 60, 66, 82, 83, 84, 85, 86, 87, 88, 89, 92, 96, 113. **Kobal Collection**: p 112/3, 114.
**Tony Mottram**: p 2, 18, 19, 20, 61, 127

Picture of Sandy Robertson on back flap also by Tony Mottram.